ORGANISATION DEVELOPMENT THROUGH TEAMBUILDING

Organisation Development through Teambuilding

Planning a Cost Effective Strategy

MIKE WOODCOCK *and* DAVE FRANCIS

Gower

Published by
Gower Publishing Company Limited
Aldershot, Hants, England

Reprints of Instruments are available. Please address enquiries to Challenge Limited, Challenge House, Victoria Street, Mansfield, Notts NG18 5SU, England.

British Library Cataloguing in Publication Data

Woodcock, Mike
    Organisation development through teambuilding.
    1. Work groups
    2. Corporations
    I. Title   II. Francis, Dave
    658.4'02   HD2741

    ISBN 0-566-02320-2

Printed and bound in Great Britain by
Biddles Ltd, Guildford and King's Lynn

Contents

Preface

As we move into the 1980s organisations are increasingly having to adjust to major upheavals. The present turbulent social and economic environment is bringing major shifts in national and international economic policies, increasingly expensive energy, threats to the productive dominance of the West, extensive technological innovation and the serious decline of many traditional industries and activities.

Those who are responsible for the management of organisations are constantly seeking ways to remain competitive, adaptable and productive despite these threats to their wellbeing. In the past twenty years behavioural scientists have helped managers to introduce the concept of planned change and a host of techniques, collectively known as Organisation Development, have been developed and tested around the world.

When we review the experience of those organisations who have undertaken a programme of Organisation Development it is apparent that the results have been patchy. Some expensive errors have been made, some unfulfilled expectations generated and some bold efforts have fizzled out as faith has deteriorated.

However, much was learned from the research and application and many useful techniques and concepts proved their value over time. One of the most significant realisations was that groups of people could be deliberately and methodically developed into effective working teams. Once developed, the team is a potent and resourceful unit which can play a vital part in creatively coping with change and innovation.

Developed teams have the following characteristics:
— They are more energetic and resourceful.

— The team style of management is positive and consistent with many of today's values.
— They encourage their members to grow and change as individuals.
— Complex problems are often solved more competently by them.
— A greater degree of commitment to change is achieved.

Teambuilding has proved to be a cost-effective and productive strategy in many organisations, but of course not all organisations have the same needs, and mechanistic prescriptions about team-building and Organisation Development generally fail. Each organisation requires an individual diagnosis and a tailor-made programme of planned change.

This book helps to develop a logical, coherent and relevant strategy for teambuilding. It is intended for use by senior managers, personnel specialists, team leaders and Organisation Development consultants. It does not make the assumption that 'teambuilding is good for you'. Rather it provides a number of tools to help collect data and evaluate the case for teambuilding.

In all organisations resources are limited and it makes sense to invest expensive time and energy where maximum benefit can be attained. We believe that teambuilding is often a valid technique but it is not the panacea for all corporate ills.

The potency of teambuilding is illustrated by the following example. The authors were consultants to an organisation employing 700 people. A thorough diagnosis suggested that the business strategy was well founded, the organisational structure appropriate and the climate positive. Yet the company was making a loss. The key problem was inadequate control and co-ordination from the senior team. A three-day off-site teambuilding session opened up all the issues and one team member said afterwards, "I'm exhausted. It was high drama. But we know what we've got to do and we'll hang on like a bull terrier." A year later the company made a small profit against a predicted loss of £¾ million. Good senior teamwork was acknowledged as the reason for success.

Most teambuilding interventions are less dramatic but the approach is no less relevant. Increasingly, those concerned with management training and development are extending their skills into the teambuilding area.

This book is structured around the key questions which we think are relevant to teambuilding strategy. Part I gives an overview and shows how an organisation development strategy can be developed. Later parts deal with each of the key questions in depth. Each topic is explained and an instrument is included which helps put the ideas into practice. However, because organisations are so complex no diagnostic instrument can be relied on to give full and complete data. The instruments in this book are meant to structure thinking and collect information, and the results should not be regarded as 'tablets of stone'. It is important to use instruments as tools in the decision-making process rather than as substitutes for it. The results need to be checked in relation to existing perceptions and common sense.

As authors of this book we have regularly used teambuilding techniques over the past ten years. We realise the potency of team-building but we also realise that it can be a high-risk strategy which when undertaken inappropriately can bring harmful consequences. Our previously published books, *Team Development Manual, Improving Work Groups, People at Work* and *Unblocking Your Organisation*, provide guidance in the teambuilding area but are principally concerned with *how to* rather than *should we*?

We are indebted to, and would like to thank, the hundreds of managers and trainers who have discussed their ideas with us and opened their teams to our research.

Any book is a snapshot in time. In a year or two we shall inevitably look over the work and realise, on the basis of further experience, that we could say some things better or differently. We hope that you will therefore consistently add your own ideas and experiences to ours. We also hope that you will find the ideas in *Organisation Development Through Teambuilding* as relevant in your work as we have found them in ours.

Mike Woodcock   Mansfield
Dave Francis   May 1981

PART I

INTRODUCTION AND OVERVIEW

TEAMBUILDING HAS been one of the most enduring themes in organisation development over the past two decades. A *team* may be simply defined as any group of people who must significantly relate with each other in order to accomplish shared objectives. *Team-building* is the process of planned and deliberate encouragement of effective working practices whilst diminishing difficulties or 'blockages' which interfere with the team's competence and resourcefulness. *Organisation development* (OD) may be defined as a process of change aimed at improving organisational effectiveness through systematic diagnosis and organisation-wide interventions.

Teambuilding has four important advantages to everyone who is concerned with the development of people in organisations:

1   Team managers and team members usually appreciate the process and almost always derive from it tangible benefits which enhance operating effectiveness.
2   The process is rapid, enduring and clearly related to organisationally significant goals.
3   Trainers and OD practitioners find that their skills are relevant and appreciated.
4   Individuals learn new attitudes and skills and improve their personal effectiveness.

When learning occurs within a working team, the benefits of new insight and improved skills can be readily put to work. Unlike many conventional training techniques, teambuilding deals with real issues and has clear relevance to organisational objectives. Also, the learning of one individual is reinforced by others in the team. We have often experienced someone returning from a training event and finding it impossible to communicate the value of the experience to colleagues. This does not happen with teambuilding as learning happens within a sub-system. The effective implementation of learning is substantially increased by taking the team, rather than the individual, as the focus of an intervention.

The case for teambuilding is clear and potent. Many working groups function poorly and fail to use the competence and ability of their individual members. Inevitably, any group takes time to become a well-integrated, resourceful and effective team but few managers recognise that they need to facilitate the process of team development. With the help of a skilful team manager and perhaps a teambuilding adviser or facilitator it often becomes possible to accelerate development towards maturity and positively to confront difficulties which would otherwise remain unresolved.

However, along with this impressive list of benefits, there are many potential pitfalls. As teams are real working units their effectiveness could be damaged by any disturbed relationships. It may be possible to walk away untouched from a group training event wih strangers and say, 'Well that was a real disaster and I hope that I'll never see any of those people again'. If anyone leaves a work teambuilding event with similar attitudes it is a serious personal and organisational problem. Teambuilding demands high trainer skills. The significance of teambuilding events adds to their drama and complexity and the facilitator often finds it difficult to tune into a new group which may have several skeletons hidden in dusty cupboards.

In recent years, several practical approaches in the field of team-building have been published and both the authors have described their own techniques.[1] However, little assistance has been available to OD practitioners in answering the question 'In what circumstances should we undertake teambuilding?'

Organisation development is a wide concept and teambuilding is only one potential component in any strategy. In our capacity as team consultants we have seen teambuilding used to great effect, but also, on occasions, inappropriately, ineffectively and unethically. Those responsible for designing organisation development strategies need a systematic procedure for examining whether teambuilding is the best choice for them. Unfortunately, there is a lack of suitable models and instrumentation to assist managers and organisation development specialists in deciding whether teambuilding is likely to be a sound investment. Accordingly, decisions taken about utilising teambuilding techniques are often taken on the basis of whim or hunch, and many organisations which could benefit from using teambuilding have ignored the potential of the approach.

The most common errors in attempting to use teambuilding as an OD strategy appear to be when:

— other more important, organisational problems require solution
— the wider organisation culture is not supportive of a team approach to management
— teams are unsuitable or unreceptive
— it is undertaken by insufficiently skilled people or with inadequate help.

These potential errors also give us criteria to assess when teambuilding would be a sensible developmental tool. We have found that teambuilding is an appropriate strategy when the following preconditions exist:

1 The lack of effective teamwork is a serious 'blockage' to organisational effectiveness.
2 The culture of the organisation supports a team approach to getting things done.
3 Teams are receptive and prepared to undertake the process.
4 Adequate resources exist internally competently to aid teams as they undergo teambuilding.
5 Adequate external resources are available if suitable internal resources do not exist.
6 Team managers and advisers are aware of the 'building blocks' of effective teamwork.

These are general themes and OD practitioners and trainers will know that a broad question is unlikely to provide the precision necessary to make a judgement on an important aspect of organisational planning. So, let us look briefly at each of the lines of enquiry suggested in the above pre-conditions, as each needs to be broken down into sufficiently differentiated topics so that hard data can be collected.

QUESTION ONE: IS POOR TEAMWORK A SIGNIFICANT
ORGANISATIONAL PROBLEM?

Organisations have varied development needs at different stages of
their history, and it is important that scarce resources are channelled
into helping the organisation cope with the challenges that it faces
at any particular time.

Managers and OD practitioners need data which will enable a
decision to be taken about the relative significance of current needs.
It has been shown to be practically impossible to work on all aspects
of personal and organisational effectiveness at the same time. Such
an approach requires an enormous commitment of resources and
may be desirable in theory but is unsustainable in practice. We have
found that a fruitful strategy is to identify two or three key areas for
thorough and sustained development effort. The Organisational
Priorities Survey (Chapter 2) provides a straightforward and comprehensive way of beginning to collect data and identify key areas on
which to work. It has the advantage of specifically differentiating
teamwork as a distinct and measurable component in a survey. Data
are provided on the relative significance of each of the eight factors
listed in Table 1. Against each factor are listed several OD techniques which have shown themselves to be useful in aiding the
blockages to be cleared.

Table 1
Some interventions

Blockage	Focus of OD intervention
1 Unclear aims	Management by objectives; corporate planning processes; communication strategies; systematic problem solving.
2 Unassertive leadership	Assertion training; gestalt groups; leadership theory and skills; team manager role analysis.
3 Ineffective management processes	Systems analysis; decision making; audits; organisation and methods studies; open systems planning; cybernetic modelling.
4 Negative climate	Survey feedback; systematic diagnosis; value clarification; motivation programmes; transactional analysis.

(continued)

Blockage	Focus of OD intervention
5 Inappropriate structure	Socio-technical analysis; contingency theory; bureaucratic models; 'small is beautiful' research.
6 Unbalanced power relationships	Conflict management; negotiation skills; social class models; confrontation theory; third party consultation.
7 Undeveloped individuals	Job analysis; training plans; personal goal planning; 'unblocked boss' approach; action learning; counselling; personal growth experiences.
8 Ineffective teamwork	Team diagnosis; structured experiences; open systems planning; teambuilding; interpersonal skill training.

Table 1 describes just a few interventions for clearing potential blockages in the people system of an organisation. Following our principle that effective OD requires that only two or three issues can be worked on at any one time, it is logical that factor 8, ineffective teamwork, must emerge as a priority for a teambuilding strategy to be justified.

QUESTION TWO: DOES THE CULTURE OF THE
ORGANISATION SUPPORT A TEAM APPROACH?

Once the decision is made that teambuilding is a significant organisational problem, it becomes necessary to decide where to start.
Organisations are complex networks of overlapping teams some of
which are temporary or relatively insignificant. Few organisations
bother to identify all of their teams, as convention suggests that
individual role holders are the units by which things get done.

The first step is to audit key teams within the organisation and
we have found it helpful to categorise them in the following way.

Top teams: Senior management groups responsible for largely
autonomous sectors of organisational operation. They determine policy and have major areas of discretion.
Management teams: Groups of managers who report to a team-
leader who is responsible for a definite area of work.
Project teams: A group formed of people who make a distinctive contribution to the accomplishment of a defined objective.
The team members report to various managers, and the team
has a defined life expectancy. Matrix teams are included.
Work teams: A group which interacts directly with products
manufactured or services provided. The team includes both
managerial and non-managerial people and behaviour is strongly
influenced by the technical systems operating.
'Standing' multi-disciplinary teams: A group formed of people
with a spread of experience which exists to meet a functional
need rather than to accomplish a specific objective. The team
may continue to operate for many years and adapt its role and
constitution as circumstances change.

The audit process begins by identifying teams and categorising
them under the headings suggested above. Then certain teams need
to be selected for more detailed consideration. The criteria we use
at this point should enable us to highlight those teams whose competent functioning is particularly significant for the organisation.
Inevitably, some teams are more valuable to the organisation than
others, and we have found it useful to allocate a crude rating to each
team using the criteria set out in Table 2.

We have now outlined a method of assigning significance to the
teams under audit but lack an assessment of their present level of
competence. Team effectiveness may be seen as a reflection of the

Table 2
Assessing team's significance within the organisation

Team's importance rating	Type of team
100 per cent	Highly inter-dependent team which is collectively responsible for achieving major objectives which have a significant effect on profitability or effectiveness. Team members must work well together to achieve results. Survival of the organisation would be prejudiced by failure.
80 per cent	Inter-dependent team which needs to be effective and competent to perform role. Makes a significant contribution to organisational effectiveness. Poor performance would lead to wasted opportunities and low morale.
60 per cent	A team which has clear objectives but can achieve success without high levels of inter-dependent working. Team members have distinct roles which have individual responsibilities and their contribution to the team is that of an 'expert'.
40 per cent	The team exists but its performance as a team only has a minor impact on the success of the enterprise. Team development would however benefit morale and motivation.
20 per cent	A loose grouping which lacks a shared objective and is organisationally relatively unimportant. Competence has little relationship to team effectiveness as individual performance is the key factor.
0 per cent	Not really a team at all. Members contribute as individuals or would be better placed in a different team structure.

current state of maturity of the group. Each work group undergoes relatively predictable changes as it progresses from an unintegrated collection of individuals to a close and effective unit. It is helpful to see this as a process of maturation. The OD practitioner and trainer needs to have a comprehensive model of maturity to assist in the evaluation. We use a five-stage approach which is summarised below.

Stages of team maturity

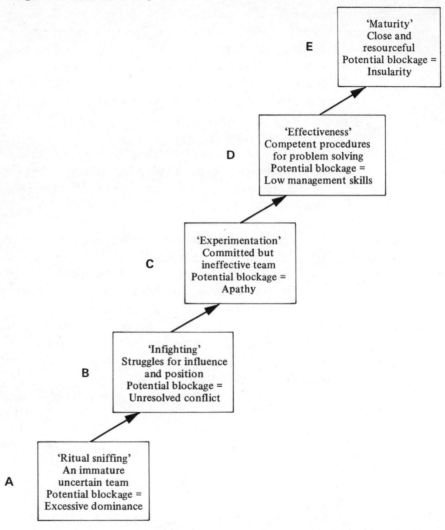

Each team can be assigned to one of the five stages of maturity outlined above and this gives the final measure we require. Sometimes a team ceases to develop under its own natural momentum. The causes of this rigidity may be described as blockages to team maturity and represent issues which the team consultant will wish to expose and help resolve.

Having assessed the stage of development of each of the teams under review and also the need for effective teamwork from an organisation perspective we now have the necessary information to take decisions about where investment in teambuilding should be made. Clearly, this will be a factor both of the stage of development and the need for effective teamwork. The decision logic is summarised in Table 3.

Table 3
Assessing priorities for investment in teambuilding

Stage of team maturity	Importance of team effectiveness	Priority
Low	Low	Low
Low	High	High
Medium	Low	Low
Medium	High	Medium
High	Low	Low
High	High	Low

QUESTION THREE: IS THE TEAM READY FOR
TEAMBUILDING?

Teambuilding is a highly effective but confronting technique. Not all teams are ready to undertake a process of teambuilding even though there may be a strong organisation case for developing effectiveness in a particular unit. We need to establish whether a particular team is suitable to embark on a systematic and deliberate process of team-building. This requires that we establish detailed criteria for assessing readiness for teambuilding.

The following questions provide us with comprehensive information which enables a decision to be made about the appropriateness of a teambuilding intervention. Typically, these questions will be worked through with key members of the potential client system to develop a consensus decision on development procedures.

1   Is the team prepared to devote time to developing competence and relationships?
2   Does the team have a budget to spend on teambuilding?
3   How much does the team manager want to develop his/her team?
4   How much do the team members want to develop their team?
5   Do team members have basic training in interpersonal skills?
6   Does the team's task require close team working?
7   Is the team manager generally held in high esteem by team members?
8   Does any member of the team have first-hand experience of teambuilding?
9   Is there an experienced teambuilding adviser available from within the organisation?
10 Does the team have access to a competent external team-building specialist?
11 Does the team have the opportunity to meet and resolve outstanding issues?
12 Is there top management support for a team approach?

It would be desirable to be able to answer 'yes' to each of these questions although, in practice, qualified positive answers are more usual.

A team which exhibits few of the basic pre-conditions is not well prepared for teambuilding and so will need considerable help and support. Alternative development strategies may be more appropriate and personal development and counselling for the team manager is frequently required.

As the 'readiness' of the team grows, so the teambuilding approach can become more directly focused on roles, work problems and personal relationships. Preparatory team training may be needed to develop a sound foundation prior to teambuilding in practice.

QUESTION FOUR: DOES THE ORGANISATION HAVE A COMPETENT TEAMBUILDER?

In many organisations teambuilding is either unknown or relatively experimental and many teams need the help of a catalyst to facilitate their team development programme. We have suggested that team-building is a highly potent but delicate intervention. Accordingly, it is very important that anyone undertaking the role of teambuilder has adequate knowledge and skill to discharge the role competently and ethically. As team techniques are relatively new, it is often necessary for those who wish to promote the approach to undertake a personal development programme. The components of teambuild-ing competence are summarised in Table 4.

Table 4
The teambuilder's audit

Competence	Outline criteria
1 Theory background	Reading of basic texts.
2 Team growth model	Familiarisation with comprehensive model of team maturity.
3 Organisational acceptance	Has legitimised team techniques within the organisation.
4 Flexible approach	Is capable of responding to diagnosed needs.
5 Repertoire of 'lecturettes'	Is able to give wide range of short talks.
6 Clarifying goals	Has skills in setting and clarifying objectives.
7 Structured experiences	Has wide range of structured experiences available and tested.
8 Realistic resourcing	Only undertakes achievable assignments.
9 Process feedback skills	Competent in mirroring back group processes.
10 Permission	Conscientiously seeks permission prior to assignments.
11 Work relevance	Makes links with real objectives and performance.

(continued)

Competence	Outline criteria
12 Co-facilitating experience	Trained in parallel with more experienced teambuilders.
13 Inter-team competence.	Skilled at improving inter-team relations.
14 Personal openness	Exhibits spontaneity and an open approach.
15 Regular review	Gets feedback and reviews own skills.

Developing competence as an internal teambuilder is a multi-facetted development need which covers theory base, techniques, skills, values, personal influence and organisational position. Each aspect requires specific attention as overall competence is a function of broad capacity in each area. The apprentice teambuilder would be well advised to audit his or her own skills and abilities and focus attention on the least developed areas. Once a basic competence level has been achieved, it is necessary to continue to be open to new methods in this developing field. We can expect to see considerable advances in team development theory and technology in the coming decade and it is recognised that current methods are crude in some respects. Each practitioner should therefore be able to innovate and develop new concepts to suit the needs of his or her situation.

We have found that competent teambuilders often share a similar approach which can be summarised in what we call our teambuilders charter. This suggests that would-be teambuilders should:

— establish clear aims
— start modestly
— ensure agreement prior to action
— build realistic time-scales
— consult widely and genuinely
— relate teambuilding to organisational work
— face up to 'political' problems
— encourage openness and frankness
— not raise false expectations
— re-organise work if necessary
— remember the unknown is often more threatening than the known.

- remember development is basically self-regulated
- remember 'you can take a horse to the water but you cannot make it drink'
- remember those who are not part of the action
- remember teambuilding can bring other problems
- be alive to other opportunities when teambuilding
- delegate
- accept external help if necessary
- learn from mistakes
- practice what is preached.

QUESTION FIVE: DO WE NEED EXTERNAL HELP?

Many organisations seek to become free of external consultant assistance as they recognise that competent internal resources offer a more significant contribution to overall effectiveness. However, external teambuilding consultation is particularly useful in one of these three situations:

— as a vehicle for development of internal resources
— to provide credibility and expertise that is not yet present within the organisation
— in facilitating the development of very senior teams whose status precludes the use of internal resources.

A competent consultant can help with many problems which confront a team. Initially there is a natural apprehension in setting out on an uncharted course. In particular team managers may feel exposed, especially if they feel that 'nasties' may lie underneath the surface. As the team develops it becomes more adept at recognising needs and process problems; however, the more objective perspective of an external agent can do much to focus issues and 'flush out' latent problems. Particularly difficult or sensitive issues occasionally occur and call for mature skills to facilitate resolution. Even a mature team may find it beneficial to have access to an external consultant. This gives the opportunity to test effectiveness and resist the enemies of insularity and complacency which can undermine close groups.

Selection of an appropriate consultant requires a systematic enquiry into two areas:

1 *What kind of needs do we have?*
How are we sure we have a teamwork problem?
Do we need outside help in further defining our teambuilding needs?
Who within the organisation has the competence to plan and run teambuilding events?
Do our internal teambuilders need help and counsel to increase their skills?
Are our internal resources sufficient in quantity and quality to meet the demand?
Do we need the stature and experience of an outside consultant to deal with particularly senior teams?

Would some of our teams benefit from the objective and impartial position of an external building consultant?

Do some teams need a high level of openness and confrontation which can best be given by an external consultant?

What objectives would we set for, or with, the teambuilding consultant?

How could we use the consultant's skills to benefit our organisation in other ways whilst working on the teambuilding assignment?

How much money are we prepared to budget for the project?

What would be the characteristics of an effective consultant for us?

Where should we look for a suitable consultant?

How many consultants should we meet as part of the selection procedure?

2 *What does the potential helper have to offer?*
What teambuilding experience does he or she have?
Do we know anything about his or her reputation?
Is he/she really interested in understanding our particular problems?
Is he/she likely to try to sell us a solution inappropriate to our needs or wishes?
Is he/she likely to make us think and act differently?
Will he/she be acceptable to our people?
Is he/she likely to set realistic objectives?
How are we going to judge success or otherwise?
Who or what is going to be developed by the project?
What is the likely cost in terms of fees?
What is the likely cost in terms of our effort?
Whose interest is the consultant likely to follow — his/hers or ours?
Does he/she have the time to devote to us?
Are we likely to be able to disengage from him/her easily when we want to?

QUESTION SIX: WHAT ARE THE BUILDING BLOCKS OF EFFECTIVE TEAMWORK?

When the case for team development has been proven, the key teams identified and shown to be ready, and competent resources have been allocated, the process of teambuilding can begin. The question is 'how?' Typically, teambuilding begins with a thorough diagnosis of current strengths and weaknesses within the team. This requires a framework for systematic assessment and we prefer the building blocks approach[2] which highlights nine distinct aspects of performance and separately evaluates a team on each factor.

These are the nine building blocks briefly described:

1 Clear objectives and agreed goals — every team member is clear about the aims of the team and committed to their achievement.

2 Openness and confrontation — people have honest relationships, identify problems and work them through to a constructive conclusion.

3 Support and trust — team members go out of their way to help each other and are able to rely on the integrity and good intent of other members.

4 Co-operation and conflict — effort is devoted to working together to resolve problems and differences of view are valued as useful aids to progress.

5 Sound procedures — work methods and problem solving are effective, with clear communication between participants.

6 Appropriate leadership — the team manager adopts a progressive and appropriate leadership style which meets the needs of individuals and helps the team to develop.

7 Regular review — the team takes time to evaluate its behaviour and learn from error or inadequacy.

8 Individual development — team members are stretched and increase their skills and stature through membership.

9 Sound intergroup relations — relationships with other groups are friendly, open, co-operative and free from destructive competition.

NOTES

[1] Woodcock, M., 'Team Development Manual'; Francis, D. and Young, D., 'Improving Work Groups', University Associates, 1979.

[2] See 'Team Development Manual', Mike Woodcock, Gower, 1979.

PART II

IS POOR TEAMWORK A SIGNIFICANT ORGANISATIONAL PROBLEM?

1
Is teambuilding a priority for your organisation?

Many organisations have attempted to diagnose their current strengths and weaknesses prior to undertaking a programme of planned development and change. Unfortunately, many managers, personnel specialists and others who have responsibility for developing a systematic framework for assessing organisational effectiveness are:

- unclear about their current organisational problems
- lacking in 'hard data' to assess current levels of effectiveness
- vague in specifying how they wish to develop in the future
- unspecific about managerial values and style
- unable or unwilling to facilitate proper debate and discussion between managers about the problems which are being faced
- developing action plans which are weak or inadequate.

Organisational problems are often difficult to grasp as they tend to be intangible and to defy measurement. Many managers have real difficulty in recognising and defining the nature of the problems or weaknesses which they are experiencing and these problems tend to continue unabated unless or until they are clearly identified and responsibility for effecting change is allocated. Organisations require, initially, a vehicle for sharing perceptions and for beginning the process of systematic diagnosis. This should enable those responsible for organisational change to take an impartial and broad view and so perceive organisational strengths and weaknesses more clearly.

The Organisational Priorities Survey in Chapter 2 has been specially designed to provide data about the organisation which are clear, concise, relevant and usable. It provides a format to facilitate collection of individual perceptions and their presentation under recognisable and useful headings. In particular, teamwork within the organisation is distinctly recognised and separately assessed.

The survey asks people to think of practical events and incidents which have happened within their own experience. This data is then used as the basis of a straightforward assessment that managers find easy to understand and use as a basis for action planning. The survey provides a basis for making rational decisions about the direction and comparative value of different strategies for planned change. Essentially it helps answer these eight questions:

1   Should we improve our planning processes and communication of objectives?
    and/or
2   Should we emphasise the development of effective and assertive leadership?
    and/or
3   Should we upgrade our management processes, control systems and communication procedures?
    and/or
4   Should we try to develop a more positive climate characterised by openness and high energy?
    and/or
5   Should we re-examine our management structure?
    and/or
6   Should we attempt to change the power balance between 'workers' and management?
    and/or
7   Should we emphasise personal, job and career development of individuals?
    and/or
8   Should we develop effective teamwork?

Because you are reading this book the final question on teamwork is most likely to concern you at present. However, it is important to emphasise that the Organisational Priorities Survey is a tool which is widely useful across an organisation and which gives significant data for planning and monitoring any process of organisation change. Prior to using the survey we suggest that you read the briefing notes which give important information on administration.

INTERPRETING THE RESULTS

The survey provides a comparative assessment of the current strengths and areas for development of the part of the organisation under review. There are eight 'effectiveness areas' which need to be understood by those analysing the results of the survey. However, we suggest that the following descriptions of the eight effectiveness areas are not read beforehand by those people completing the survey, as insight into the categories can bias the final results.

AREAS OF ORGANISATION EFFECTIVENESS

1 Clear aims

All organisations, even partnerships, are formed with the intention of achieving results which no one person could attain individually. Many resources, systems, talents and energies are brought together to provide a capability to achieve results by producing products or services.

It is vital that organisations clearly identify what they wish to achieve and devote their resources to accomplishing specific goals. However, the wider environment is constantly changing. New opportunities and threats come bubbling to the surface and require decision and redefinition. As a general rule it is true to say that when an environment is harsh or turbulent then organisations need very clear goals and stricter emphasis on concrete achievement.

Many organisations lack adequate methods for clarifying their aims and communicating these across the organisation. This results in unfocused effort, unnecessary competition, 'empire building' and demoralised teams.

When an organisation is strong at clarifying and communicating aims we see the following characteristics:

- Individuals and teams are skilful in clarifying objectives and presenting them clearly.
- The organisation is able to re-define objectives in the light of new information and events.
- Sectional interests, special needs and unusual difficulties are integrated within an overall framework of objectives.
- Objectives and broad aims are clearly communicated across

the organisation in terms which relate to day-by-day responsibilities.
– Criteria for success are defined and monitored.
– Organisational objectives are related to wider social and
economic needs.

When an organisation has unclear aims it needs to embark on a
process of re-examining existing planning processes, developing skills,
developing better communication techniques and working to set
higher standards of clarity.

2 Assertive leadership

Over the centuries many authorities, writers, managers and statesmen
have tried to identify the qualities of successful leadership. Some
pundits emphasise human qualities such as honesty, integrity, fairness or courage. More recently we have seen attempts by behavioural
scientists to measure the differences between successful and unsuccessful leaders using complex scientific techniques. Organisational scientists tend to describe leadership in terms of 'correctly
identifying the needs of subordinates for direction and support and
skilfully meeting these needs in the pursuit of organisational objectives'. An effective leader is a person who 'successfully influences
others to pursue goals energetically and effectively'. These
definitions enable us to see that leadership is a function which is
active and directed towards achievement.

The concept of 'assertive leadership' helps to emphasise the point.
Assertion may be defined as 'knowing what you want, refusing to be
side-tracked and vigourously moving towards your goals'. This
stance is distinct from aggression which involves the use of force and
unethical pressure in an attempt to dominate or win.

In many organisations those in a position of responsibility see
their jobs as being chiefly concerned with co-ordination and decision
making. This view of leadership is often inadequate as enterprises
thrive on risk-taking, vigorous responses and a strong drive towards
excellence.

Competent and assertive leadership is important at all stages of
an organisation's growth. Often, in adverse times there is a tendency
towards demoralisation and defeatism which, if allowed to continue

unchecked, undermines organisational effectiveness. Without assertive leadership the vitality and quality of the organisation deteriorates rapidly and it becomes unable to cope in a competitive and harsh environment.

Some of the key problems of unassertive leadership are:

- insufficient internal questioning and review
- low morale and demoralisation
- slow response to problems and opportunities
- poor standards of performance
- lack of risk taking
- excessive workload for senior managers
- emphasis on bureaucratic systems.

Organisations which take steps to develop the capacities of those in leadership positions are building a resource which is capable of constantly initiating and sustaining change. This may involve training, appraisal, counselling and reinforcing competent leadership behaviour by rewarding achievement.

3 Effective management processes

Organisations develop systems and procedures to co-ordinate effort and monitor accomplishment. The behaviour of people within organisations is partially conditioned by the responsiveness and quality of these systems. In one case we saw a flourishing business being allowed to wither and die simply because the senior team lacked the information necessary to make essential decisions. In this organisation, despite frantic efforts and long hours of worry, the absence of sound decision making procedures resulted in organisational errors, lost opportunities and mounting losses which became unsustainable. As an ashen-faced accountant announced the latest financial losses the senior team reviewed their unsuccessful efforts with one member remarking 'we should never have put to sea in a leaky boat'. The analogy is excellent. Attempting to manage an organisation with undeveloped management processes is similar to sailing a ship with defective rigging and leaks. So much energy needs to go into keeping afloat that there is little left to focus on real achievement.

Ineffective management processes have the following consequences:

- poor co-ordination
- excessive bureaucracy
- inadequate standards of control
- risk of abuse, theft and nepotism
- waste of managerial time
- build up of frustration and irritation
- ponderous and lethargic decision-making
- an atmosphere of frantic activity which has been well described as 'running about like a headless chicken'.

The development of effective management processes, which increasingly use modern technology, is a crucial aspect of organisational effectiveness. Improving managerial processes requires professional review, use of advanced communication technology and training.

4 Positive climate

All organisations and many units within organisations develop a distinctive character or climate. This is a unique blend of personalities, systems, attitudes, history, physical environment and setting. The climate within an organisation is very influential in determining how individuals feel about things, how they relate to each other and perhaps most important, how much energy they are willing to expend in pursuing organisational goals.

In one organisation we know the climate could have been described as friendly and paternal for two generations. The basic product range was in demand and stable, procedures and conventions became established and, like the changing of the Guard at Buckingham Palace, became traditions. Then a technological breakthrough quickly made the existing product range out-dated. It was fascinating, although alarming, to observe the way this tradition-bound enterprise tried, but failed, to grapple with managing innovation although it had sufficient financial backing to develop and enter new markets. Their climate was too tradition-bound for the decisive and innovative approach which was needed.

A negative climate acts like a resistance movement in an occupied country. Although disguised, there are many major and minor acts of sabotage which undermine the established order, and constrain the organisation from making good use of its potential. The following characteristics usually accompany a negative climate:

- low levels of trust and openness
- lack of concern for organisational goals
- people are not generally helpful or supportive
- departments and groups develop 'political' or 'win–lose' relationships
- difficult problems are evaded
- blame is allocated and used as a weapon
- a low level of confidence and morale
- low energy levels.

Developing a positive climate is a painstaking task that is made more difficult because the results are hard to measure objectively. However, a negative climate is a continual drain on corporate effectiveness and needs skilful and methodical development. The adage 'If you're not part of the solution, then you're part of the problem', is often particularly relevant when it comes to developing a more positive climate.

Improving organisation climate is a difficult assignment as many factors interact together. Top management attitudes, physical and social environment, management style, systems of production, and business fortunes all have their influence. Often a systematic review of organisational climate is a sound basis for a development programme.

5 Appropriate structure

Organisation structures enable the diverse talents and resources of an organisation to be channelled towards performing tasks which are often difficult, complex or tedious.

Organisations usually have a hierarchy of power and responsibilities with channels of communication and control already developed. Charts are sometimes prepared which identify functional areas, key relationships and roles, and specifications of expected behaviour are written. All of these things in themselves distinct from the personalities involved, can be described as the organisation structure.

The search for an ideal structure has been largely abandoned. Different technologies and the stage of evolution of the enterprise profoundly affect the decision about which structural option to choose. For example, six kinds of organisation can be identified with each needing a specific type of structure to meet its needs.

Craft The organisation has to produce largely individual items which must be separately planned and constructed. The tasks require adaptive skills and many technical decisions.

Batch   A number of products or services are produced, but once a line is established then a run is maintained for a period of time. Repetitive work is combined with skilful performance.

Process   A small number of products are made on a continuous flow. Jobs may be highly responsible, but are governed by rules and procedures. Little innovation occurs on a day-to-day basis.

Dispersed   Sometimes units are geographically spread, for example with a chain of distribution depots or retail shops. Here local management have some initiative to adapt their operation to take account of local circumstances. There is the possibility of expressing flair and some autonomy.

Creative   Organisations may be specifically set up to manage innovation. They become very dependent on harnessing personal talent. Organisations can be structured around a brilliant researcher, or resourceful teacher. Fluid organisational systems are needed to cope with change.

Temporary   Certain organisations are established for a limited time (eg, to produce a film), and then are disbanded. They need rapidly to become effective and produce a high standard of professional output despite setbacks.

Each of these different kinds of organisation requires a particular structure to cope with its specific demands. Of course, a large organisation will include several of these kinds within it, and hence we frequently see communication difficulties between apparently competing units.

Decisions about structure are never easy. Strong arguments can always be made for different options. However, if a structure is created which does not suit the system or technology it can produce severe disadvantages. For example:

- poor decision-making
- inadequate co-ordination
- overload of some managerial levels
- long response time to problems
- insufficient personal and career development opportunities.

Developing an appropriate structure is a key senior management role. It requires a comprehensive understanding of the work tasks which need to be undertaken, together with some knowledge of relevant behavioural research.

6   Balanced power relations

In recent decades we have seen the rise of shop floor power and ever-increasing demands for more democratic decision-making in work organisations. Changes in the balance of power within organisations have presented many problems for management who have found themselves increasingly vulnerable to pressures from organised labour. During this period organisations have increasingly been using more advanced technology which has often left them even more vulnerable to disruptive action by employees. Many enterprises have declined in their adaptability and profitability as a direct result of the erosion of managerial initiative and influence.

The balance of power within organisations is an intensely political issue which is debated at government level, at political party level, in the boardroom, on the shopfloor and in the home. Those of a socialist persuasion claim that elitism and unfair privilege are the primary causes of industrial unease. Others, towards the right of the political spectrum, feel that the growth of industrial democracy is a creeping disease which saps the vitality of managements. It is clear that there are no finite solutions which are guaranteed to resolve power issues in any organisation. Much depends on the prevailing political climate within the wider society, on legislation, real or pending, and most of all on the attitudes and stances of those involved.

Once it is recognised that unbalanced power distribution is a significant problem within an organisation the remedy is likely to be complex and painful. Many strategies have been attempted and the risks of failure are high. A hard-line approach designed to increase managerial initiative can lead to negative confrontations and humiliating defeats. Softer approaches which promote power-sharing, greater communication and collaboration can result in neutered decision-making, unwieldy participative structures and low productivity. Improving unbalanced power relationships needs assertive initiatives from management. This can only come from a clear stance on managerial philosophy and values. Top management need to be very clear about their concept of a healthy organisation and realistic about the steps needed to accomplish necessary changes.

7   Developed individuals

Organisations are combinations of individuals, and in the final analysis personal competence is the most important area of organisational effectiveness.

People who are new to the organisation need to be quickly brought up to a basic standard of competence and those who have been in the organisation for some time will require an up-dating of their knowledge and skills to keep abreast of changes in methods and technology.

In addition to technical and job related skills there is the wider issue of personal and career development. We have identified eleven managerial effectiveness areas:

1   Self management competence —
    being able to make the most of one's time, energy and skills. Being able to cope with the stresses of present day managerial life.
2   Clear personal values —
    having a set of values which have been deliberately chosen and are appropriate to working and private life in the 1980s.
3   Clear personal goals —
    skilfully setting personal targets which help self-development, meet material and career aspirations and provide a balance between work and private life.
4   Continuous personal development —
    working to develop personal insight, ability and stature in order to rise to new challenges and opportunities.
5   Adequate problem-solving skills —
    having the right skills in individual and group problem-solving and decision-making.
6   High creativity —
    being able to generate new ideas and put them into practice.
7   High influence —
    making a significant impact on others; being listened to and gaining commitment to ideas and proposals.
8   Managerial insight —
    understanding the motivation of others and skilfully employing appropriate leadership techniques.
9   High supervisory skills —
    having the practical ability to achieve results through the

efforts of others.
10 High trainer capability —
being able to help others to develop their skills, judgement, maturity and competence.
11 High teambuilding capacity —
developing and using the potential of teams to achieve results unattainable by individuals.

Although managerial jobs differ from each other in the demands they make, each of these eleven effectiveness areas is potentially important to any manager. Improving individual performance begins for the manager with an analysis of strengths and weaknesses. Organisations can then help create appropriate learning opportunities, although we believe that most personal development is the ultimate responsibility of the individual.

8 Effective teamwork

Ever since the Stone Age, when men gathered together in hunting bands to provide food for themselves and their families, people have found work teams a natural and resourceful way of getting things done. We see teamwork in every area of life from a hospital operating theatre to an infantry unit.

Unfortunately, many potential teams fail to develop as effective units. This largely results from managers being unaware of the benefits of teamwork and unskilled in the techniques of developing effective working groups. When a team is working well it is a highly resourceful, energetic unit which sustains individual morale and combines differing personal strengths into a powerful group. The word *synergy* has been coined to describe this special blend of energy and competence.

An effective team will show the following characteristics:

- It will establish and work towards clear objectives.
- It will have open relationships between members.
- It will deal with different viewpoints and gain from debate.
- Members will show a high level of support for each other.
- Personal relationships will be based on personal knowledge and trust.
- People will want to work together to get things done.

— Potentially damaging conflicts will be worked through and resolved.
— Procedures and decision-making processes will be effective.
— Leadership will be skilful and appropriate to the needs of the team.
— It will regularly review its operations and try to learn from experiences.
— Individuals will be developed and the team will be capable of dealing with strong and weak personalities.
— Relations with other groups will be co-operative and open.

Each of these aspects of team effectiveness can be developed and in Chapter 6 we describe them in greater depth.

The organisation which fails to develop the competence of its teams loses an important resource. Organisations which identify the need to develop team competence also need to convince everyone concerned of the potential value of teamwork, and provide the necessary skills and support to enable teambuilding to take place.

In summary, the organisation effectiveness areas are:

1 Clear aims

The organisation has carefully defined its objectives and ensures that these are well communicated throughout. Individual managers relate their work to corporate goals and people clearly understand the mission of the organisation.

2 Assertive leadership

Those in managerial positions adopt an assertive and vigorous approach and take a positive leadership role. They adopt an entrepreneurial approach which emphasises achievement and problem-solving.

3 Effective management processes

Systems and procedures are carefully designed to provide control without inhibiting initiative or flexibility.

4 Positive climate

Attitudes and relationships are, on balance, friendly, co-operative, open and positive. People make efforts to help each other and assist the organisation to achieve its objectives.

5 Appropriate structure

The hierarchical structure of the organisation is suitable to the tasks being completed and assists work to be effectively completed.

6 Balanced power relations

The relationships between management and worker groups have been resolved so that the managerial function retains initiative and decisiveness and yet operates with fairness and integrity.

7   Developed individuals

People have skills to perform their current jobs well and their individual potential is developed.

8   Effective teamwork

Groups work well together and resources are co-ordinated effectively. Meetings achieve useful results and projects are accomplished by multi-disciplinary groups.

2
Organisational Priorities Survey

In order to assess whether the development of teamwork is a priority for an organisation it is necessary to answer the broader question 'What development needs does the organisation have at this time?'

The Organisational Priorities Survey helps to do this by collecting subjective opinions, clarifying options and assisting senior management to evaluate 'the state of the nation'.

When using the survey it is important to work within the following guidelines:

- Obtain as wide a spread of participants and data as possible.
- Beware of increasing expectations and then frustrating them.
- Provoke discussion about the results in order to validate them.
- Consider the results as indications rather than as scientific facts.
- Influence those with organisational power seriously to consider the findings.
- Move towards action and remedy rather than repeated diagnoses.

THE SURVEY – HOW IT IS CONSTRUCTED

The survey is in two parts. The first part is used for the collection of data, and the second part, which may or may not be used with respondents provides an explanation of the outcomes. The survey uses a forced choice design. This has the advantage that all of the

key areas are compared with each other so that a comparative
priority is established. However, the survey design does not in itself
indicate the magnitude of problems and senior managers will still
need to take the final decision as to where decisive action is needed.

In completing the survey respondents are asked to compare several
pairs of statements and assess their relative weight, and it is important that a short briefing is given which emphasises that the survey is
designed to identify priorities and that whilst choices are often difficult to make, they are necessary if development resources are to be
used wisely.

HOW TO USE THE SURVEY

The survey asks managers and others with a viewpoint on the organisation to record their views. In our experience it takes people about
fifteen or twenty minutes to complete the survey form. It is important that the process of data collection is managed carefully as simple
errors in procedure can invalidate the results. We suggest that the
following steps are taken:

Step 1

Define the part of the organisation you wish to survey. This may be
a department, function, site, project group, company or the total
organisation. It is essential that everyone completing the survey is
considering the same 'unit' and this should be clearly stated on the
front of the survey form. People should only be asked to survey
those parts of the organisation with which they have personal contact.

Step 2

Consider preparing a briefing statement which identifies the purpose
of the survey and describes the uses to which the data will be put.
It is important to ask for truthful views and to try to ensure that
false expectations are not aroused.

Step 3

Try to collect viewpoints from a broad and representative sample of
informants. Different levels within the hierarchy usually have distinct

viewpoints and it is important that all perspectives are represented. Some organisations may choose to collect data anonymously.

Step 4

Ensure that those responsible for change work through the results in detail. Real action is usually stimulated by deeper review and discussion.

Step 5

Use the survey again to review progress over time. A periodic assessment is a valuable tool in monitoring progress.

Step 6

Decide whether the survey will be scored by the respondent or by someone centrally. When self scoring is used the respondent is issued with Parts 1 and 2. When central scoring is used the respondent is only issued with Part 1.

INTERPRETING THE RESULTS

After scoring, each of the eight factors will have a score between 0 and 21. The total numbers of points allocated between the eight factors is 84. The higher scores indicate organisational problems and are likely to be priorities for a programme of planned change. Lower scores represent organisational strengths. The scoring sheets included in Part 2 enable an individual to complete the survey and interpret his or her personal result. Where the survey is completed across a team, the data can be further analysed using the suggested format overleaf.

	Tom	John	Mary	Peter	Andrew	Jane	TOTAL	PRIORITY
1	Unclear aims							
2	Unassertive leadership							
3	Ineffective management processes							
4	Negative climate							
5	Inappropriate structure							
6	Unbalanced power relationships							
7	Undeveloped individuals							
8	Ineffective teamwork							

IS TEAMWORK A PRIORITY?

Assuming that the survey has been conducted in order to determine whether organisational resources should be invested in improving team effectiveness, it is necessary to look at the comparative position of factor 8, Ineffective Teamwork. In our experience if this does not feature as one of the first three priorities for action, the organisation is likely to gain more benefit from putting resources into an area with a higher priority. However, the management group themselves must take the decision and a comprehensive discussion of the results greatly aids the chances of an accurate diagnosis, as well as increasing commitment to any development programme.

ORGANISATIONAL PRIORITIES SURVEY – PART 1

This survey invites you to think about the organisation you work in and to contribute to increasing understanding of what needs to be done to strengthen it in the future.

The first step is to be clear about which part of the organisation you are considering. You may be surveying a department, function, site, company or total enterprise. Write a definition of that part of the organisation in the space below, we will call it the *unit*.

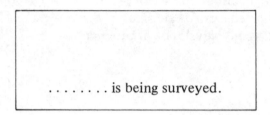

Now, in respect of the unit described above *only*, consider each of the statements below. You are asked to consider the relative importance of two statements. You have three points to allocate between each of the two statements. If you consider one to be very important and the other unimportant then you can allocate all three points to the important item. Alternatively, you can allocate two points to one choice and one point to the other. The options are:

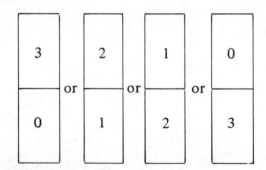

The purpose of the survey is to identify priorities, so sometimes you may find it difficult to make a choice between the options – but choices are a necessary part of working life! If you wish to make any further comments write them in the space at the end of the survey.

1

A	
B	

It would help if people were much clearer about the aims of the organisation.

Effective leadership is lacking.

2

C	
D	

There is a significant waste of resources.

People seem to be generally 'switched off' by working here.

3

E	
F	

The way the organisation is structured causes problems.

Relations between management and labour are often difficult.

4

G	
H	

Many people are not fully competent at their jobs.

Teams often fail to achieve their potential.

5

B	
C	

Many managers lack entrepreneurial flair.

Systems are often cumbersome and ineffective.

6

D	
E	

There is a lot of destructive 'political' behaviour.

The organisation would benefit from a thorough revision of roles.

7

F	
G	

Management have lost some of their capacity to manage effectively.

Individuals lack skills in tackling their own jobs.

8

A	
C	

Objectives need to be much more clearly spelt out.

Some important managerial systems fail to take advantage of new technology.

9

B	
D	

A significant number of key managers lack leadership flair.

The atmosphere in the organisation lacks energy and a feeling of urgency.

10

C	
E	

Procedures often inhibit work being done quickly.

Reporting relationships are confused.

11

D	
F	

On the whole people are not sufficiently interested in their work.

Management and workers do not have co-operative relationships.

12

E	
G	

Some levels of management are largely unnecessary.

There are insufficient skills among key employees.

13

A	
D	

Corporate plans are poorly communicated.

There is a lack of friendly openness between people.

14

B	
E	

On the whole managers lack assertion and drive.

The 'chain of command' is excessively long.

15

C	
F	

Systems for decision-making need to be overhauled

Fear of worker reaction inhibits much useful change.

16

D	
G	

Many people are negative and disheartened with their work.

Individuals are not being developed sufficiently to meet the long term needs of the business.

17

E	
H	

The organisational structure is not appropriate for our needs.

Meetings are frequently unconstructive.

18

A	
E	

Objectives are frequently stated unclearly.

The organisation structure does not encourage rapid response to problems.

19

B	
F	

An entrepreneurial approach to leadership is lacking.

It would be true to say 'power is abused in our organisation'.

20

C	
G	

Managerial systems tend to inhibit creativity.

Many individuals have an out-of-date concept of their job requirements.

21

D	
H	

People tend to avoid talking openly to each other.

Co-ordination between people working together is often lacking.

22

A	
F	

Aims are too varied and vague for people to identify with.

Powerful cliques control much of what happens.

23

F	
H	

Conflict between powerful groups wastes resources

Project groups seem to work slowly.

24

B	
G	

Those in positions of leadership rarely command full respect.

Individuals have failed to achieve much of their potential.

25

C	
H	

A review of methods and systems would be most helpful.

A team approach would aid morale and effectiveness.

26

A	
G	

Some senior managers fail to communicate their goals clearly.

Certain key skills are lacking in the organisation.

27

B	
H	

Those in managerial positions have not learned fully how to develop their leadership capacity.

Individuals tend to work alone and not share problems.

28

A	
H	

A comprehensive statement of overall objectives would be useful to many people.

We are slow at getting projects completed and using the skills of individuals.

SCORING

Now go back over your scores and total each separate letter. Write the totals in the boxes below:

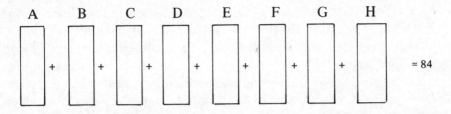

Check! Does the total of all eight boxes equal 84? If not, you have made an error, so please look again at your scores.

FURTHER COMMENTS

I would like to make the following points . . .

ORGANISATIONAL PRIORITIES SURVEY – PART 2

EXPLANATION OF RESULTS

The questionnaire examined eight areas of organisational effectiveness in order to provide a basis for discussion and ultimately for establishing priorities for further development of the unit.

Most people find it helpful to see the results in chart form. From the final page of Part 1 of the survey transfer your scores to the chart opposite. Circle the number which represents your score on each scale. Connect the circled points to complete a profile which gives you visual feedback on the potential strengths and weaknesses of your unit as you see them.

You have now analysed the results of the Organisational Priorities Survey and obtained a comparative assessment of the strengths and weaknesses of the unit in relation to the eight effectiveness factors described below. A high score in any area suggests that it could be a priority area for development. Here is a short description of the eight effectiveness factors.

1   Clear aims

The organisation has carefully defined its objectives and ensures that these are well communicated throughout. Individual managers relate their work to corporate goals and people clearly understand the mission of the organisation.

2   Assertive leadership

Those in managerial positions adopt an assertive and vigorous approach and take a positive leadership role. They adopt an entrepreneurial approach which emphasises achievement and problem solving.

3   Effective management processes

Systems and procedures are carefully designed to provide control without inhibiting initiative or flexibility.

4   Positive climate

Attitudes and relationships are, on balance, friendly, co-operative, open and positive. People make efforts to help each other and assist the organisation to achieve its objectives.

ORGANISATIONAL PRIORITIES SURVEY – SUMMARY CHART

Unclear aims	Unasser- tive leader- ship	Ineffective manage- ment processes	Negative climate	Inappro- priate structure	Unbalanced power relation- ships	Undevel- oped individuals	Ineffective teamwork
21	21	21	21	21	21	21	21
20	20	20	20	20	20	20	20
19	19	19	19	19	19	19	19
18	18	18	18	18	18	18	18
17	17	17	17	17	17	17	17
16	16	16	16	16	16	16	16
15	15	15	15	15	15	15	15
14	14	14	14	14	14	14	14
13	13	13	13	13	13	13	13
12	12	12	12	12	12	12	12
11	11	11	11	11	11	11	11
10	10	10	10	10	10	10	10
9	9	9	9	9	9	9	9
8	8	8	8	8	8	8	8
7	7	7	7	7	7	7	7
6	6	6	6	6	6	6	6
5	5	5	5	5	5	5	5
4	4	4	4	4	4	4	4
3	3	3	3	3	3	3	3
2	2	2	2	2	2	2	2
1	1	1	1	1	1	1	1
0	0	0	0	0	0	0	0
1	**2**	**3**	**4**	**5**	**6**	**7**	**8**
Clear aims	Assertive leader- ship	Effective processes	Positive climate	Appro- priate structure	Balanced power relations	Developed individuals	Effective teamwork

Now:

List below your three highest scores   List below your three lowest scores

| 1 |
| 2 |
| 3 |

| 1 |
| 2 |
| 3 |

5   Appropriate structure

The hierarchical structure of the organisation is suitable to the tasks being completed and assists work to be effectively completed.

6   Balanced power relations

The relationships between management and worker groups have been resolved so that the managerial function retains initiative and decisiveness and yet operates with fairness and integrity.

7   Developed individuals

People have skills to perform their current jobs well and their individual potential is developed.

8   Effective teamwork

Groups work well together and resources are co-ordinated effectively. Meetings achieve useful results and projects are accomplished by multi-disciplinary groups.

You should now be in a better position to decide on eight key questions:

1   Should we improve our planning processes and communication of objectives?
     and/or
2   Should we emphasise the development of effective and assertive leadership?
     and/or
3   Should we upgrade our management processes, control systems and communication procedures?
     and/or
4   Should we try to develop a more positive climate characterised by openness and high energy?
     and/or
5   Should we re-examine our management structure?
     and/or
6   Should we attempt to change the power balance between 'workers' and management?
     and/or
7   Should we emphasise personal, job and career development

for individuals?
and/or
8 Should we try to improve our teamwork?

PART III

DOES THE CULTURE OF THE ORGANISATION SUPPORT A TEAM APPROACH?

3
Key teams: their stage of development and relative importance

Strategic decisions about teambuilding require an awareness of the current needs within the organisation. This involves identifying and auditing the key teams and making well-considered choices about which teams should benefit from any investment in teambuilding.

This chapter is concerned with how to examine methodically each of the key teams in an organisation and then plan a team-building strategy based on it conducted by senior management and/or personnel specialists.

THE TEAM REVIEW GROUP

In our experience the review is best carried out by a group of senior managers and/or personnel specialists who have a strategic overview of the organisation. Accordingly, it is often useful to form a 'team review group' consisting of such people. This group needs to be able constantly to refer to those with a broad understanding of the organisation, its development needs and its likely changes in operation. It goes without saying that this team may need some development itself to work effectively! The procedure which the group should follow is described as a series of steps although in practice the steps may not be sequential.

STEP 1: IDENTIFYING KEY TEAMS

Every organisation can be viewed as an interconnecting network of teams. One way of usefully dividing them is into the following categories:

> *The top team*: The senior management group collectively responsible for key decisions and policy guidelines.
> *Management teams*: Groups of managers who are responsible for a definite area of work, reporting to a team manager.
> *Project teams*: Groups formed for a particular purpose in which the members do not report to the senior person.
> *Work teams*: Those involved in actually accomplishing tasks. Including both managerial and non-managerial people.
> *Multi-disciplinary teams*: A group combining a spread of experience which establishes guidelines and resolves issues of principle. Different from a project team in that the remit is broader.

Clearly some other definition or grouping of teams can be used but it is important that every important section of the organisation is reviewed in order that the key teams can be identified.

STEP 2: ASSESSING THE STAGE OF DEVELOPMENT

Teams almost invariably develop through a series of stages as they progress from an immature collection of individuals to a closely integrated and effective working group. During this period procedures, methods of operation and team climate undergo tremendous changes.

Any attempt at defining these stages, and the changes associated with them must be an over-simplification. However, we have found that a straightforward model based on five stages of development is very useful in helping to review organisational teams and determine which are likely to be the most receptive to change.

The principle we utilise is this: if a team needs to work effectively but is inhibited from doing so by being at too low a stage of development, then it is ripe for teambuilding investment.

In order to make this assessment teams need to be categorised on the five stage model (Table 2). Evaluations will necessarily be somewhat crude; however, the purpose is to conduct a broad assessment, and detailed study of team functioning will be conducted later.

Here is our description of the five stages of team development.

Stage A: 'ritual sniffing'

Whenever animals come together there is a period of testing out and getting acquainted. A similar process exists when new teams are formed. People seek to identify their place in relation to others. However one characteristic of teams at this stage is that feelings and genuine emotional reactions are usually kept hidden. People tend to conform to the established line, partly because they are apprehensive of suggesting changes. The person in a position of authority is central, and people watch to see how far it is possible to 'rock the boat'.

Meetings often consist of a series of statements with people queueing to put their point of view without listening to what goes before or afterwards. Often little care is shown towards other people or their views and that is frequently characterised by a lot of talking and little real listening. Personal weaknesses tend to be covered up because the group lacks the skill to support or eliminate them. Mistakes are used as 'evidence' to help convict people rather than as opportunities to learn. There is often only a shallow understanding of what needs to be done, and objectives are poorly set and communicated.

Politeness and order are the best that can be expected at this stage. However, this condition is only skin-deep. Difficulties related to inadequate procedures, inter-personal difficulties and uncertain commitment lurk, like minefields, waiting to emerge. This tends to occur in stage B.

Stage B: 'infighting'

As the team develops it becomes important to sort out personal relationships and clarify power and authority relationships. The team manager has particular status because his position has been recognised by the organisation and the trappings of influence have been allocated to him. Yet this position has to be earned. Team members carefully watch and evaluate their manager's performance. They may accept leadership gladly or find cunning ways to avoid it.

Relationships between team members become more significant. Alliances are formed and cliques often form. Certain individuals become liked and respected by others. Other people find that their colleagues are irritating or unacceptable. Animosities, expressed more or less politely, rise to the surface. Commitment to the work of the team is often a major issue. Some individuals may use the group for ulterior motives, with some devious personal strategy underlining apparently civilised behaviour.

Teams comprising both men and women are especially interesting at this stage. Elements of sexual competitiveness are frequently present. Although there may be no intention to act on sexual attractions, they are rarely absent. People compete for attention and wish to be seen as especially attractive or powerful. Sex is an extremely energising and motivating force in many teams and organisations and issues of sexual attraction, repulsion or indifference sometimes need to be worked through.

Development through the infighting stage occurs with deeper inter-personal knowledge and the building of a group climate which enables people to express their differences and find common understanding. The integrity and overall unity of the team becomes more important than individual gratification.

Stage C: 'experimentation'

This stage begins when the team decides that it wishes seriously to review its operating methods and undertake activities to improve its performance. The team becomes willing to experiment; to sail in 'uncharted waters'. Problems are more openly faced and the underlying values and assumptions affecting decisions begin to be debated. More risky issues are opened up and often the way the group is managed is an early topic for discussion. More personal issues are raised, feelings respected and personal animosities dealt with. This may lead to some traumatic encounters between team members, but the quality of their relationship is sufficient to support individuals through upheavals.

The team becomes more inward-looking, and for a time may reject other individuals or groups. This is a transient phase in which the energy of the group is devoted to solving its own problems of relationship and effectiveness. The quality of listening undergoes marked improvement. Functioning within the team can become uncomfortable but also dynamic and exciting. The observer can see things coming to life and people who have been dormant for years beginning to contribute.

However, the team still lacks the capacity to act in an economical, unified and methodical way. Some inter-personal issues have been resolved and there is a climate which supports individuals and gives energy to the next stage — the search for effectiveness.

Stage D: 'effectiveness'

The team now has the confidence, open approach and trust to examine its operating methods. Generally the team needs to look at the procedures and problem-solving skills it uses to conduct its business. These have to be reviewed in substantial depth. Each person in the team needs to contribute to framing the methods to be used. Frequent review is required to provide the data for improving effectiveness.

The work of the team becomes identified with precision, contributions are clarified and improved and clear objectives are set. Team members become concerned with economy of effort and task effectiveness. The team becomes more competent to handle problems creatively, flexibly and effectively. Without this attention to its working methods the team will continue to use marginally effective modes of operation and satisfy itself with an adequate performance, rather than striving for excellence.

As the team works through this stage, it becomes genuinely proud of its capacity to achieve. Results improve and recognition comes from other sources. Team members value their involvement more, protecting the team from threats to its well-being. Gradually the team grows in competence and resourcefulness. Membership takes on a real significance for everyone concerned and the final stage – maturity – is reached.

Stage E: 'maturity'

By now the team has achieved the openness, concern and improved relationships of stage C and the effective working methods of stage D. Maturity means that the team can develop open relationships with other groups and flexibility becomes the keynote. Procedures are adopted to meet different needs, leadership is decided by the situation and not by protocol. The group itself recognises the kind of leadership which is necessary and the leader recognises the need to involve the team in matters of substance. Everyone's energies are utilised for the benefit of the team. There is a strong sense of pride in the achievements of the team and a satisfying relationship between members. However, each individual's needs are identified and met as the team is genuinely concerned with the well-being of each person.

The team is responsive and responsible as it considers essential principles and the social aspects of decisions. It realises that it is part of a larger organisation and has social and moral responsibilities. Trust and openness, co-operation, confrontation and a continual review of results become part of the way of life. The desire to develop means that competent outside help is welcomed.

The team is not only admired, but it is emulated by others. The team is a happy and rewarding place to be. The bonds of comradeship are often so close that they exist beyond the business life of the team. Informality characterises the group but this is based on positive regard for each other. Roles of individuals are clear and each person's contribution is important and distinctive. A mature team does not allow its function to become redundant or obscure; it influences others to give recognition and support.

STEP 3: NEED FOR EFFECTIVE TEAMWORK

Inevitably some teams are more significant or indispensable to the organisation than others. The purpose of this step is to estimate the importance of effective teamworking for each team. We find a sliding scale useful in making this assessment, and we use the definitions of the need for effective teamwork set out in Table 5 opposite.

It is possible to assign a rating for each team under review, using the 0, 20, 40, 60, 80 and 100 benchmark definitions for guidance.

STEP 4: IDENTIFYING PRIORITY TEAMS

Having assessed the stage of development of each of the teams under review, and also the need for effective teamwork within each team, it is now possible to take decisions about where investments in teambuilding should be made. Clearly, this will be a factor both of the stage of development and of the need for effective teamwork. For example:

- A low stage of development and a low need for effective teamwork will mean a low priority.
- A low stage of development and a high need for effective teamwork will mean a high priority.
- A high stage of development and a high need for effective teamwork will mean a low priority.
- A high stage of development and a low need for effective teamwork will mean a low priority.

Table 5
The need for effective teamwork

Need rating	Type of team
100 per cent	Highly inter-dependent team which has to achieve as a team to a very high standard to maintain organisational effectiveness. Major effect on profitability, and survival would be prejudiced by ineffective team-working.
80 per cent	Inter-dependent team which needs to be above average in team effectiveness. It must make a significant contribution to organisational health and profitability.
60 per cent	Important team which has to make a competent contribution. Some inter-dependence amongst team members means that contribution could not exclusively come from individuals.
40 per cent	Team exists but does not make an indispensable contribution to profitability or survival as a team. Further team development would mainly benefit morale.
20 per cent	A loose grouping which makes little vital contribution as a team and which has working practices which do not necessarily require a team method of working.
0 per cent	Not really a team at all. Members could contribute just as well to organisation effectiveness as individuals.

4
Teambuilding Priorities Assessment

PURPOSE

This instrument is designed to help decide where to begin a team-building programme.   All organisations can be seen as inter-connecting networks of teams.   Some teams are by definition or membership more important or significant to the effectiveness of the organisation than others.   Also some teams are more developed than others either because they have undergone teambuilding activity previously or because their maturity or work methods are more conducive to effective teamwork.   This instrument is designed to help would-be teambuilders to decide which teams should have the priority for teambuilding effort.

INSTRUCTIONS

Decide who is to complete the instrument.   Remember that the results will be more accurate if a group of people who have a strategic overview of the organisation co-operate.   Those who are to complete it should first read Chapter 3 on key teams and refer to it as necessary throughout.   Work through the instrument step by step.

ESTABLISHING TEAMBUILDING PRIORITIES

STEP 1

Turn to the Teambuilding Priority Worksheet (p. 66). Identify all of the teams which you wish to review. You must include all of those teams which you consider to be key to the success of your organisation. Remember:

- top teams
- management teams
- project teams
- work teams
- multi-disciplinary teams.

List them in column 1 by title — if they don't have a title give them one for the purpose of this review.

STEP 2

Consider the Stages of Team Development — Summary Chart (p. 67) and assign to each key team identified in column 1 a letter or pair of letters which indicate the stage of development of that particular team. Not all of the characteristics of a particular stage will be relevant to any one team at any time — the intention is to identify whch of the 5 stages *best* represents the position of the team. If you feel that a team is genuinely between two stages then use two letters, e.g. A—B.

STEP 3

In column 3 on the Teambuilding Priority Worksheet, *for each team* assign a percentage ranking for 'organisation reliance on team effectiveness'. Remember that it is *importance of teamwork* which is being reviewed and *not* contribution of individuals. The more inter-dependent the team members are the higher will be the rating.

Use Table 5 (p. 61) for reference.

STEP 4

In column 2 we now have an estimate of the stage of team development of each team and in column 3 we have a measure of the importance of effective teamwork within each team. Using this information now rank in column 4 the priority for team development activity. This will be a factor of both the stage of development and the need for teamwork.

The teams with the high priority are the ones where teambuilding investment is likely to bring the greatest rewards.

Teambuilding Priority Worksheet

(1) Title of key team	(2) Stage of development	(3) Need for effective teamwork	(4) Priority for team development

Table 6
Stages of team development — summary chart

Openness, concern and improved relationships of stage C. Effective working methods of stage D. **PLUS**	Informality and respect. Success emulated by others. Happy and rewarding. Outside help welcomed. Open relationships with other groups. Flexibility. Leadership decided by situation. Pride and satisfaction. Individual needs recognised and met. Social aspects considered. Trust, openness, co-operation, confrontation. Continual review of 'way of life.	*Stage E Maturity*
Operating methods examined. Procedures reviewed. Problem solving skills developed. Frequent review. Clear objectives. Search for economy. Problems handled creatively. Team pride. Members protect team.		*Stage D Effective- ness*
Not working in unified way. Not working in methodical way. More dynamic and exciting functioning. Dormant people begin to contribute. Review of operating methods. Performance improvement activities undertaken. Willingness to experiment. Values and assumptions debated. Risky issues opened up. Leadership or management discussed. Personal animosities dealt with. Inward-looking. Better listening.		*Stage C Experi- mentation*
Team leader performance evaluated. Relationships more significant. Alliances and cliques formed. Personal strengths/weaknesses known. Commitment debated. Interest in climate. Team needs come to the fore. Differences expressed more openly.		*Stage B Infighting*
Testing out. Feelings kept hidden. Conforming to established line. Apprehensive of change. Authority central. Little listening. Little care for others. Personal weaknesses covered up. Mistakes used as evidence. Objectives poorly set. Objectives poorly communicated.		*Stage A Ritual sniffing*

DIRECTION OF TEAM DEVELOPMENT

PART IV

IS THE TEAM READY FOR TEAMBUILDING?

5
Readiness for teambuilding

Teambuilding can be an effective and economic use of resources. Learning and development is carried out within the working group and there are many opportunities to improve everyday relationships and effectiveness. Unlike some conventional training techniques, teambuilding deals with real issues and enables groups to make practical advances.

However, not all teams are ready to begin teambuilding. The approach requires that certain preconditions are met. Three questions need to be asked:

– Do team members want to engage in teambuilding?
– Could the team cope with the demands of teambuilding?
– Does the organisation support a teambuilding approach?

The instrument Teambuilding Readiness Survey has been designed to help assess whether a particular team is suitable for a teambuilding approach. Each of the items on this instrument has a direct bearing on the likelihood of success and we comment on each in the explanatory notes below.

1 Teambuilding takes time

The teambuilding approach requires that people learn new skills, work through relationship problems and review current effectiveness. This all takes time to complete thoroughly. If a team is not prepared to spend time 'contemplating its own navel' then it simply lacks the will or drive to develop itself. In practice, significant steps can be made within a two-day period but a comprehensive teambuilding approach may take much longer.

The decision to spend time on teambuilding is an important test of commitment.   If the approach is valued the group will take steps to ensure that significant progress is made.

2   *How much money is available for teambuilding?*

Another test of commitment is the willingness to spend money on teambuilding projects. Much can be achieved on a low budget, but the willingness to spend money is a good test of team interest. It is a particularly significant statement of how much the group values the approach.

Teambuilding is often helped by the services of a skilled adviser. Some organisations have suitably qualified people on their staff, in other cases an outside consultant is used. Such a person may not be easy to find, and will expect a high professional fee for his work. Also there are costs which will inevitably be incurred: hotels, transportation, training materials and time.

3   *Does the team manager want to undertake teambuilding?*

The senior person in the team is particularly important. He or she will often be confronted with difficult feedback and so must be willing to undertake the activities and be open to the teambuilding process.

Without definite and clear enthusiasm it is virtually impossible for teambuilding to get off the ground. This energy and commitment needs to be based on a realistic understanding of teambuilding. Occasionally managers agree without understanding what they are inviting to happen. Later they get cold feet and withdraw, leaving the team in a worse condition than previously.

Team members look to their leaders to give a lead. Usually they will tailor their own reactions to make them appropriate and acceptable. The team manager's informed, open and positive stance is a very significant aid to success.

4   *Voluntary involvement of team members*

Through bitter experience we have found that it is important to ensure that all team members are prepared to involve themselves in teambuilding. This does not have to be a wholehearted commitment as reservations from inexperienced participants are both natural and reasonable. However, there must be a willingness to try teambuilding and be open about doubts and concerns.

If any team member is opposed to the teambuilding approach they can sabotage any activity. We feel that it is unethical to put excessive pressure on any individual. Often reservations or opposition are based on fear and it is important that this is dealt with prior to teambuilding activities.

A commitment from all team members is a necessity and their enthusiasm a great advantage.

5 Training in inter-personal skills

In recent years many competent training programmes in inter-personal skills have been developed. When a team contains members who have experienced such programmes there is a reservoir of skills which will increase the possibility of rapid progress.

Such individual training is a useful foundation for teambuilding and is particularly helpful with people who have difficulties in relationships or communication.

6 Standing of the team manager

Team leaders who enjoy respect and loyalty and are highly valued by their groups are in a good position to develop the team, as support is already present.

Team leaders who are less well considered need to recognise that part of the process of teambuilding will include an open, probably uncomfortable, evaluation of their own role. This can lead to a positive outcome if feedback is taken and changes made. However, should the team manager act defensively and spurn comment there is a strong probability that the outcome will be negative.

7 Substantial task

Teams which respond best to teambuilding are those with a substantial and important task to be accomplished. Only if the team has a need to be effective will it be seriously interested in becoming so. The most effective teambuilding sessions are those which help members work together more effectively and this results in clear improvement in team performance. Without a substantial task the team often ceases to be a working group and so lacks the will to forge itself into an effective unit.

8   Teambuilding experience

When one or more team members have previously experienced team-building in practice they act as catalysts and help the process to develop more quickly.   To the uninitiated teambuilding appears somewhat mysterious and perhaps like a minefield.   Previous experience helps people to realise the potential of teambuilding and to support others as they go through the process.

9   Competent internal help

Teams quite often need help whilst undertaking teambuilding. Like any management technique the team approach needs to be learned, considered, experienced and applied. A competent team trainer can do much to help teams to understand the teambuilding process. Also he or she can act as a catalyst, observer, tutor and process consultant whilst teambuilding sessions are in progress.

Organisations which have a strong and competent person to help teams develop are much better equipped to undertake teambuilding. Occasionally teams can get into troubled waters. Difficulties may emerge which the group finds it impossible to resolve. It is impor-tant that someone should be available to assist the team if it gets stuck in this way.

10   Competent external help

Some consultants have specialised in team effectiveness, working in many different organisations. Their professionalism can be a useful aid. The team benefits from a depth of experience, more comparative data, an incisive approach and the objectivity that comes more easily from an independent person.   This can be especially useful with senior groups who may respond better to an external consultant when there is no one within the organisation with the capacity to overcome internal resistance.

Sometimes it is useful for an external teambuilder to support the work of an internal specialist and this can be an effective way of developing in-company competence.

11   Regular meetings

Teambuilding is a process for developing working groups who have shared tasks. Without regular meetings there is no basis for the growth of the informal relationships which characterise an effective team. One of the most potent benefits of the team approach is the group vitality which develops and sustains individual members. This takes time to build and requires meetings and events to create a positive climate. From joint activity comes commitment to team achievement.

12 Top management support

Managers are influenced in their style by the attitude and approach of the top management group. Organisations where the team approach is understood and supported by top managers have a more favourable climate for teambuilding. This encourages those involved who feel that the approach they are taking is legitimate and supported.

Without top management support it is harder for the individual manager to employ the technique although useful work can still be undertaken. The success of teambuilding can influence others in the organisation to take the approach seriously.

13 Importance of team to organisation

It makes sense to begin a teambuilding approach with significant groups whose effectiveness makes a substantial impact on the well-being of the organisation. In most organisations teambuilding competence is a scarce resource and so the use of this potent technique is best applied to significant teams.

THE CRITERIA AND INSTRUMENT

The thirteen criteria identified in the Teambuilding Readiness Survey and in the explanation are intended to help assess whether a particular group is 'ripe' for the approach. You will notice that some of the criteria are weighted as being more important than others. These weightings, given a numerical significance in the instrument, are based on the considered views of experienced teambuilding consultants. They are meant to help you and the team make choices but the real test is — does the team really want to plunge in?

6
The Teambuilding Readiness Survey

PURPOSE

Teambuilding efforts have more success where the ground is fertile. This instrument is designed to help determine whether the team under review is likely to be receptive to teambuilding activities by considering particularly whether it is worth developing a particular team, whether the team could cope with the demands of teambuilding and whether the wider organisation is supportive of a teambuilding approach.

INSTRUCTIONS

Complete the survey and then total your individual scores.

TEAMBUILDING READINESS SURVEY

1   Is the team able and willing to devote time away from day-to-day pressures to developing effectiveness?

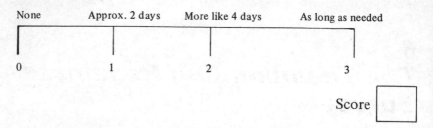

Score ☐

2   Is the team prepared to spend a budget on teambuilding?

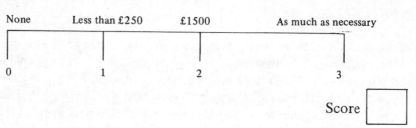

Score ☐

3   Does the team manager *want* to build his/her team?

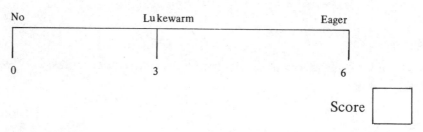

Score ☐

4   Do team members *want* to build their team?

No   Lukewarm   Eager

0   3   6

Score ☐

5   Do team members have training in inter-personal skills?

No	Some members	All
0	2	4

Score [ ]

6   Is the team manager respected and accepted by the team?

Little	Somewhat	Greatly
0	3	6

Score [ ]

7   Does the team have a substantial work task which requires that they work together to achieve objectives?

No tasks in common	Some shared tasks	Substantial task
0	3	6

Score [ ]

8   Does anyone in the team know about teambuilding methods first hand?

No one	Someone
0	3

Score [ ]

9 Is there an experienced teambuilding adviser available from within the company?

No   Yes   Outstandingly competent

0   3   5

Score

10 Does the team have access to an external resource to aid team-building?

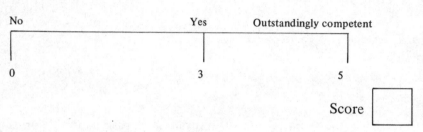

No   Yes   Outstandingly competent

0   3   5

Score

11 Do the team have regular meetings?

No   Monthly   Weekly or more

0   4   6

Score

12 Do top management support a team style of management?

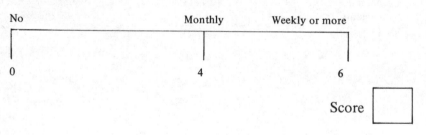

No   Yes

2   6

Score

13 Is the team's task important to the organisation as a whole?

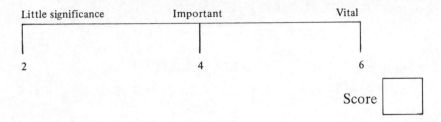

Little significance   Important   Vital

2   4   6

Score

SCORING

If the total of your score is:

less than 25:
The team is not well prepared for teambuilding and so will need considerable help and support. Other development strategies may be more appropriate. A thorough diagnosis and evaluation of the options is required.

25—45 points:
The team is probably ready to begin preparatory work prior to teambuilding. This includes training in inter-personal and problem-solving skills, insight into group development and leadership style.

more than 45 points:
The team is well prepared to use a task-related teambuilding approach.

PART V

DOES THE ORGANISATION HAVE A COMPETENT TEAMBUILDER?

7
Skills and approach of the competent teambuilder

Teambuilding can be a cost-effective and powerful way of developing people within organisations but the services of a catalyst or teambuilder are frequently required. Sometimes external help may be necessary but in many cases a competent internal adviser is enough to assist teams to become competent and resourceful.

The teambuilder's audit enables you to think about two vital aspects of the teambuilder's contribution; the knowledge and skills required and the general approach adopted. When you have considered both aspects it can be useful to prepare a personal development plan for yourself which will help you to develop your skills and approach more systematically.

THE KNOWLEDGE AND SKILLS OF THE COMPETENT TEAMBUILDER

1   Background reading in teambuilding theory

In recent years several books and articles have been written about teambuilding. These provide many useful ideas and techniques. As teambuilding is a powerful intervention into the life of a working group it is vital that the process is carried out thoroughly and carefully. Background reading aids competence and confidence, thereby reducing the risk of unproductive sessions.

2   Theory of team growth

Teams go through a gradual process of growth from an initial immature stage to a smoothly functioning and close working group.

It is important that the teambuilder has a realistic model of the stages of development (see p. 67) which enables the present level of effectiveness to be accurately diagnosed. Further development of the team can then be soundly planned using appropriate inputs, projects and experiences.

3   Repertoire of 'lecturettes'

One way for the teambuilder to assist the team is by giving short talks, or 'lecturettes', which focus attention on relevant areas for development. The skillful teambuilder will have developed a repertoire from which can be drawn useful material to cover the range of difficulties which may be encountered.

4   Availability of structured experiences

Large numbers of exercises, projects and activities have been developed to help individuals and teams learn, from experience, about effective group working. These 'structured experiences' are vital to effective teambuilding and the competent teambuilder will have acquired experience in using a number which help groups overcome their difficulties.

5   Skill in process feedback

One of the most important jobs of the teambuilder is to act as a mirror to the group and reflect back the characteristics of its present methods of operation. This requires careful observation of the processes in the team and the capacity to give accurate and useful feedback. The team then use this information, plus their own observations, to monitor their effectiveness and identify areas for improvement.

6   Personal acceptability

The successful teambuilder needs to have the personal skills to gain rapport with a group and be respected as a useful and trustworthy adviser. The team is entrusting confidential and delicate matters into their teambuilder's hands and they need to have trust in his or her integrity and competence.

7   Co-facilitating experience

The teambuilder's skill is developed by working with competent and experienced practitioners. In this way the skills of designing team-building events can be learned. In particular, the competent team-builder needs to gain experience of knowing when to introduce new inputs and experience and of the skills of timing. These things can best be learned through working with an experienced teambuilder.

8 Personal openness

Skilful teambuilding requires an open approach to dealing with issues which are important to the development of the group. These may often be sensitive and uncomfortable. The competent team-builder will have developed a capacity to identify topics needing to be aired and will have the skills to confront issues openly. Some-times individuals need to receive feedback on the effects of their own behaviour and this requires similar skills of personal openness.

THE APPROACH OF THE COMPETENT TEAMBUILDER

A TEAMBUILDER'S CHARTER

1 Organisational acceptance

> Ensure teambuilding is understood.
> Build support for your work.
> Acquire resources for teambuilding.

2 Adopt a flexible and open approach

> Collect information about the team's needs.
> Start modestly: success builds confidence.
> People are more comfortable with things they can grasp.
> Things are less threatening when they are openly discussed.

3 Clarify goals carefully

> People are often wise about their needs.
> Do not raise false expectations.
> It often pays to record goals.
> Be prepared to change direction.

4 Be realistic

> Start modestly: 'big oaks from little acorns grow'.
> Agree realistic time scales: 'Rome was not built in a day'.

'Unlearning' often needs to precede learning.
'Cultural' changes come slowly.
Accept external help if necessary, as it can offer impartial expertise.
Face up to 'political' pressures.

5   *Get permission to work*

Commitment grows from real understanding.
Change without commitment is empty.
Check commitment before starting teambuilding: consultation is not a chore, it is essential.
Manipulation undermines teambuilding.
Development is basically self-regulating.
People *cannot* be forced into attitude change.
People *cannot* be forced into openness and honesty.
People *can* often be manipulated into pretending to change.

6   *Make relevant to everyday work*

Beware of too many 'games'.
Work may need to be reorganised.
Look at the team's day-to-day effectiveness.
Examine delegation and decision-making.

7   *Build good contact with other teams*

Plan specific changes.
Use regular meetings to build teams.
Remember that teambuilding can make other groups feel insecure.
Some people may feel excluded.
Poor inter-group relations are often wasteful.
Clarify how the team will relate to other teams.

8   *Regularly review your competence*

Admit it when you are wrong.
Review progress regularly.
Encourage feedback.

Honest feedback is a valued gift.
Develop your integrity and openness.

The skills and the approach of the competent teambuilder can usefully be linked together in the Teambuilding Competence — Summary Chart, below.

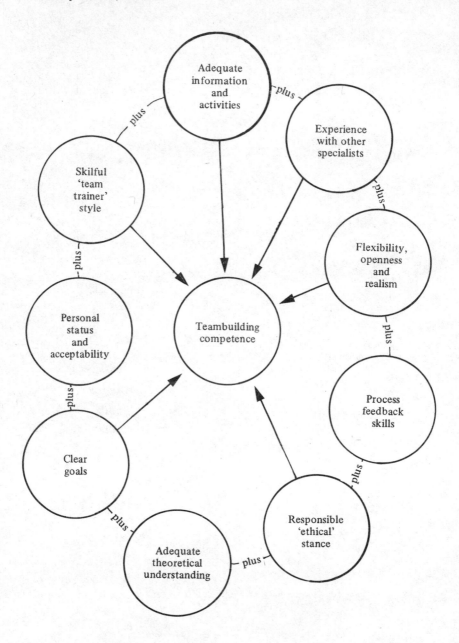

8
The Teambuilder's Audit

PURPOSE

The audit can be used to assess your own skills and approach as a teambuilder.

INSTRUCTIONS

Work through the questions in the audit putting a mark on each scale to indicate your current position. Answer all questions then complete the answer grid at the end of the instrument.

If you work with others you can invite them to fill out a Teambuilder's Audit on your behalf and use this to validate your own views, and then devise a personal development plan for yourself.

THE TEAMBUILDER'S AUDIT

1   Background reading

I have no real knowledge of
the literature of teambuilding.

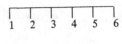

I have studied at least 500 pages
of teambuilding literature.

2   Organisational acceptance

Teambuilding is neither valued
nor understood within the
organisation.

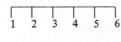

I have ensured that team-
building is both understood
and accepted as an important
strategy within the organisation.

3   Theory of team growth

My knowledge of the stages of
team development could be
written on the back of a postage
stamp!

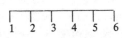

I have a clear and comprehensive knowledge and under-
standing of the usual stages of
team development.

4   Flexible approach

I follow a rigid approach when
teambuilding.

My approach varies consider-
ably with the needs of the
group.

5   Repertoire of lecturettes

I am unable to give short talks
on team development issues.

I am able to give a range of
short talks on every major
aspect of teambuilding and
effective team operation.

6   Clarifying goals

It is hard for me to help a team
to clarify its development goals.

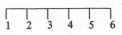

I am experienced and com-
petent at helping others to set
useful goals.

7   Availability of structured experiences

I am unaware of any exercises, instruments or techniques which could help a team to develop.

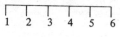

I am experienced in using a wide range of structured experiences and other team-building techniques.

8   Realism

I undertake assignments without really considering the resources required to cope.

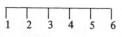

My work is always sufficiently well resourced to be effective.

9   Skill in process feedback

I am unskilled in observation and giving feedback to groups.

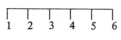

I am trained and experienced in observing team process and giving feedback.

10   Permission

The voluntary agreement of all concerned in teambuilding is not important to me.

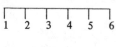

I conscientiously check that all concerned have given their permission and commitment to teambuilding.

11   Personal acceptability

There is little evidence that the organisation values my personal contribution as a teambuilder.

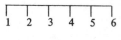

My personal contribution as a teambuilder is valued in many parts of the organisation and I am trusted.

12   Relevance to everyday work

I do not place much significance on the link between teambuilding and everyday work.

Application of teambuilding to day-to-day work is of primary importance to me.

13   Co-facilitating experience

I have never worked alongside an
experienced teambuilder or
adviser.

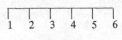

I have experienced the work
of several different teambuilding advisers and received
coaching and advice from
them.

14   Contact with other teams

Relationships with other teams
are usually ignored in my teambuilding work.

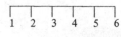

I deliberately help teams to
develop positive relations with
other groups.

15   Personal openness

Often I fail to confront difficult
or important issues openly.

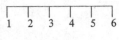

I always openly confront all
difficult and important issues
and ensure that I work them
through.

16   Regular review

I rarely review my approach to
teambuilding.

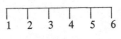

I take steps to get feedback on
my approach and regularly
review my competence.

ANSWER GRID

Question number	Your score	Total score		
1 3 5 7 9 11 13 15		} . . . Part A		TEAMBUILDER'S SKILLS
2 4 6 8 10 12 14 16		} . . . Part B		TEAMBUILDER'S APPROACH

This audit enables you to take a quick look at your teambuilding knowledge and skills (Part A) and your approach to teambuilding (Part B).

Although the instrument will only give you a subjective impression you may find it helpful to grade your scores as suggested below:

For both Part A and Part B individually

4–15 points – insufficient preparation for teambuilding work
16–25 points – major areas of development needs
26–35 points – basic competence, some development required
36–48 points – good standard of professional competence.

If your score in Part A is too low, pay particular attention to the section 'The knowledge and skills of the competent teambuilder'.

If your score in Part B is too low, pay particular attention to the section 'The approach of the competent teambuilder'.

PART VI

DO WE NEED EXTERNAL HELP?

9
The team development consultant

Although we believe in do-it-yourself approaches wherever possible, there are some circumstances in which teams do need external help in working on their own development. This chapter is about the following issues concerning choosing and working with a consultant:

- — when to use a consultant
- — what kind of consultants can contribute
- — the qualities and characteristics of a good team-development consultant
- — where to find consultants
- — how to choose a suitable consultant
- — the stages of working with a consultant.

WHEN TO USE A CONSULTANT

A consultant can help with a number of problems confronted by a team that is just beginning to consider its own development. Initially, there is the natural apprehension of the team's leaders and members in setting out on an uncharted course. Team managers may feel particularly exposed, especially if they suspect that 'nasties' may lurk beneath the surface. Some team members also may feel rather apprehensive about exposing themselves to a new and unknown process.

As their skills develop, teams usually become adept at recognising their own process problems. But at first, people may be too engrossed in what they are doing to be able to stand back and see what is going on; they can use the perspective of an external agent. And while a team is developing, problems and issues may arise that are particularly difficult or sensitive; these call for the skills of a consultant.

As a team matures, it normally develops the ability to handle its own problems and the need for external help either diminishes or disappears. Later, mature and effective teams may want to spend time with a trusted consultant once or twice a year, just to get another perspective on how things are going.

Lastly, a consultant who is known in the wider organisation can help in handling inter-group relationships.

Summary

A consultant can be used:

- to help start a team-development process
- when team managers and members do not have the skills at the same time to manage and take part in team-development activities
- when there are difficult or sensitive issues to be worked through
- when team members feel that they are too involved in issues to be able to stand back and see what is going on
- to give impartial feedback on team performance and problems
- to help a team review progress at intervals
- when inter-group problems arise which are difficult for the team to handle alone.

WHAT CONSULTANTS CAN CONTRIBUTE

A consultant cannot make a team effective; teams do that for themselves. There also is no way in which a consultant can do the work of the team. But a consultant can assist a group in many different ways.

Sometimes an organisation simply needs someone who possesses expert knowledge not contained in the organisation. Once the knowledge is transferred, there is no need for the consultant, who then is paid and leaves. At other times, there are people who possess skills that are beyond the capacity of anybody in the organisation.

A good example of this is the expert firefighters who put out oil-rig fires.

Team-development consultancy is different from the two other kinds just mentioned. It is not the *content* of the team's work that is being worked on, but the *process* by which members of the team work together. This distinction between *content* and *process* is vital.

A team-development consultant is concerned with helping the team to:

— identify blockages to effective working
— diagnose what is going on inside the team and why the blockages exist
— recognise, confront, and work through the problems themselves
— set team-development objectives, and chart their own progress.

The consultant's major contributions are likely to be:

— observing what is happening between team members as the team works
— serving as a mirror to the team, so that the members have a clear view of their behaviour
— selecting activities that are appropriate in helping the team improve its performance
— giving feedback to the team and its members on how they are doing.

A team-development consultant will not:

— usurp leadership, but will support the manager and each member
— tell the team what is wrong with it, but will help the team to recognise its own problems
— make decisions for the team, but will help the team to make its own decisions
— get engrossed and involved in the content of the team's work
— make the team dependent on his continued presence; but will work to make the team independent of external help.

Good team-development consultants can provide skills in working sensitively with groups of people in a helping and supportive way and also offer their experience in working with the problems of many teams. It is these skills and experiences that the team is buying.

QUALITIES AND CHARACTERISTICS OF A GOOD TEAM-DEVELOPMENT CONSULTANT

We know a brilliant consultant who failed high school, worked as a carpenter for fifteen years, and then by accident became involved in team-developing work. Another successful consultant started work as an engineer and, through his church membership, became involved in social work and then team-development. Another colleague has a degree in psychology and a PhD based on psychotherapy research. One of the worst failures we have encountered in consultancy has a degree in sociology and long experience in social work, clinical psychology, and research. Our conclusion is that a string of academic qualifications is no guarantee that a consultant is good.

Identifying the characteristics of effective consultants is difficult because of the wide diversity of backgrounds and experience shared by those we have known, but here is our best attempt.

An effective consultant

1   He or she is a person who has self-knowledge, gained from a breadth and depth of personal experience. This knowledge cannot be developed from text books or academic education. It comes, rather, from working extensively with other people and working through their own personal values. A consultant is likely to manifest these characteristics through behaviours such as:

- listening actively
- valuing others as people
- taking people as they are
- having space and time for working with others
- abstaining from personal crusading and dogmatic views
- clarifying his personal values
- confronting people and issues positively
- reflecting problems to people in a helpful way.

2   He or she has a foundation of practical theory. This does not mean an ability to regurgitate other people's theories, impressive though this may seem. It does mean that the individual is able to draw on research and theory in a relevant way to guide his or her work.

3   He or she is open and realistic. Some consultants will promise the world. Others are subtle manipulators who attempt to con or even threaten others into changed behaviours. A good consultant

will be open in giving feedback to others and will be quite explicit about his or her own values. Importantly, he or she also will develop a clear 'contract' at the beginning of a job, which will define the expectations and responsibilities of both client and consultant.

4   He or she can work with the team on the here and now issues, but also encourage the members to visualise ways of improving for the future. However, beware the consultant who lives always in the future, especially where results are concerned.

WHERE TO FIND CONSULTANTS

When an organisation has no need for a consultant, it may be assailed by publicity material promising dramatic consulting results in every field conceivable — from accounting to Zen meditation.

When there is a specific need, then finding the right consultant may become a challenge. Sometimes it seems as though all the good consultants have migrated to greener fields, are booked for the next year, or were last heard of heading for the desert to write a book.

However, the right consultant can be found somewhere — in business schools, other centres of management education, large and small consultancy firms, inside other companies, and in independent practice. Consultants work under many different titles with the commonest being: group facilitator, group-training specialist, change agent, and personal-skills specialist.

The very best way to find the right *individual* to meet your needs is by personal recommendation from people who have had good experiences. To do this, first check with companies or other organisations who have done some work in group-training or team-development.

A second approach is asking a local business school to recommend someone. If this fails to produce results, find a management publication containing material relevant to your interests. Then contact the publisher or the author to see if they know of any suitable people. If you still have no success, try the larger consultant firms that specialise in personal skills and group-training, or contact the associations of consultants and management associations that exist in most countries.

A word of warning: when approaching large institutions or consultancies, remember that you are going to work with an individual person, not the institution, so check on the person who will be doing the work.

As a last resort, define your need, write it down, send it to us and we will try to be of help.

HOW TO CHOOSE A SUITABLE CONSULTANT

It is wise, first, to check out the work of a prospective consultant and look for relevance to your needs and standards of quality. Any consultant worth his salt will be pleased to refer you to past clients; if necessary, visit them.

A second tactic is talking with several consultants and choosing one of them. Discuss your problems with each consultant and work through whatever strategy is proposed. Does it feel right? Realistic? Not too slick?

In working through these issues with you, the consultants should be showing some of the behavioural skills that will be manifest in their work. Reject a consultant such as the one who totally disrupted a whole office by his pushy and pompous telephone behaviour. When this man finally reached the manager and announced that he was a 'specialist in human relations', the manager, having heard the effects of his behaviour, just said, 'I don't believe you!' and hung up.

Another criterion is whether you feel any personal warmth, trust, and understanding developing. This is critical because a team-development consultant will be working intimately with the team and each one of its members. The initial exploration of problems with a team manager and the team (done before any commitment to work is made) should be deep enough to enable the team to develop a personal feeling of whether it would feel good about working with the consultant.

Something to check as part of the initial 'contract' with a consultant is whether he will devote sufficient time and energy to service your needs.

Finally, can you afford the consultant? Consultancy is not cheap, but a good consultant can make all the difference to the success of your team's development.

THE STAGES OF WORKING WITH A CONSULTANT

Effective management of the introduction of a consultant to your team or organisation will reduce the risks of a bad experience. The process could include the following steps:

1   Review and identify the group's needs. What issues and problems does the team feel it has? Can these be handled internally or should they be dealt with by somebody in the wider organisation? (Here the Team-Review Questionnaire from Francis and Young, *Improving Workgroups* can be of great use.)

2   Obtain consensus from the team concerning the need for an external consultant. If there is a general feeling that skilled outside help is necessary, then move to the next step.

3   Contact a number of suitable consultants and have them meet other team members.

4   Select the most appropriate consultant.

5   Develop a 'contract' with the consultant. This is not so much a formal written document as a mutual understanding that covers the following:

   — the initial diagnosis of the problems to be worked on
   — the method of working on these problems
   — how much further diagnosis is required, and how this will be done
   — the relationship between the consultant and team members (especially the team manager)
   — what kind of role the consultant normally likes to play
   — the design of initial activities
   — how progress will be reviewed
   — how success will be judged
   — when work will start
   — the time scale over which work will be carried out
   — the broad amount of consultancy time required
   — how much this will cost, and how the consultant will be paid.

6   Complete the initial diagnostic work and plan the initial activities. As much as possible, this should be done with and accepted by the whole team.

7   Start work. Review.

8   Identify how and broadly when the consultant will begin to withdraw from the team. A good consultant's major aim will be to bring the team to a position in which it is strong enough to handle its own development without external help. Make sure this issue is raised with the consultant.

At some stage in a team's growth, an outsider may be an essential agent to help unblock problems. But, in the end, the health and effectiveness of any team must be assessed by the team itself.

10
The Team Development Consultant Audit

PURPOSE

Executives and trainers can be bombarded with alleged helpers, advisers and consultants. Although the relationship between company and consultant often proves disappointing, sometimes the outcomes are invaluable. This instrument will help you get maximum benefit from your investment in consultant help.

Use Part A to consider whether outside help is required in a specific situation.

Part B should be used as a checklist to ensure that essential points are covered in any discussion with a consultant you are considering engaging.

TEAM DEVELOPMENT CONSULTANT AUDIT

PART A

Needs checklist

1   How are we sure we have a teamwork problem?
2   Do we need outside help in further defining our teambuilding needs?
3   Who within the organisation has the competence to plan and run teambuilding events?
4   Do our internal teambuilders need help and counsel to increase their skills?
5   Are our internal resources sufficient in quantity and quality to meet the demand?
6   Do we need the stature and experience of an outside consultant to deal with particularly senior teams?
7   Would some of our teams benefit from the objective and impartial position of an external building consultant?
8   Do some teams need a high level of openness and confrontation which can best be given by an external consultant?
9   What objectives would we set for, or with, the teambuilding consultant?
10 How could we use the consultant's skills to benefit our organisation in other ways whilst working on the teambuilding assignment?
11 How much money are we prepared to budget for the project?
12 What would be the characteristics of an effective consultant for us?
13 Where should we look for a suitable consultant?
14 How many consultants should we meet as part of the selection procedure?

PART B

Consultant checklist

1   What teambuilding experience does he have?
2   Do we know anything about his reputation?
3   Is he really interested in understanding our particular problems?
4   Is he likely to try to sell us a solution inappropriate to our needs or wishes?
5   Is he likely to make us think and act differently?
6   Will he be acceptable to our people?
7   Is he likely to set realistic objectives?
8   How are we going to judge success or otherwise?
9   Who or what is going to be developed by the project?
10 What is the likely cost in terms of fees?
11 What is the likely cost in terms of our effort?
12 Whose interest is the consultant likely to follow — his or ours?
13 Does he have the time to devote to us?
14 Are we likely to be able to disengage from him easily when we want to?

PART VII
BUILDING EFFECTIVE TEAMS

hotel conference suite.

THE ATMOSPHERE in the (board room) was heavy and intense. The senior managers in the organisation had received a shock. One division of the business had been expected to return a handsome profit until a recent audit revealed that basic flaws in costing would result in a substantial loss. The chief executive said, 'I don't want to be unfair but the way I feel at the moment one of you is going to be hung, drawn and quartered for this. When I was at Group Headquarters the company chairman said to me, "You've just used up six of your nine lives." So give it to me straight. Where did we go wrong?'

There was a pause and one manager said, 'Well, the problem is that no one is specifically responsible for relating cost projections to market forecasts. We operate functionally and the only person with an overall view is you Sir, as chief executive. You are the hub; we all feed information in to you and you are the only one who can make overall decisions.' The other managers nodded in agreement with this analysis of their managerial process but the chief executive said, 'You can't expect me to understand all that detail. It's your job to make the decisions work and you must have been aware that something was wrong.' There was a pause before one man cleared his throat with nervous tension and said, 'I think that several of us are nervous about highlighting problems because experience suggests that we are likely to be up to our ears in manure if we speak up.' The chief executive said, 'Well, two things are clear to me, firstly we are organised badly if mistakes like this can occur, and secondly, there needs to be much more frankness and openness in our relations with one another. How are we going to improve matters?' Go TO Page 3.

The chief executive was asking a useful question which could be re-worded as 'how can we develop as an effective working group?' Almost everyone finds themselves a member of a group which fails to identify or achieve its objectives. Group relations are frequently lifeless, defensive, ineffective, unsatisfying and confusing. This is a costly defect in any organisation since much planning and decision-making depends not just on individuals but also on group effectiveness. Managing change in a turbulent environment requires that people come together to co-ordinate resources, initiate and progress ideas, gain commitment to common goals and collectively manage complex operations.

Many managers claim to favour and practice a team approach but few have a clear understanding of what this means in practice. Only in recent years have we clearly diagnosed the characteristics of effective working groups and learned to express them in down-to-earth terms. It is now possible for a manager to develop the skills which will enable him deliberately and logically to build a team out of a dispirited and unco-ordinated collection of individuals.

Teambuilding is a conscious and deliberate process to develop the kind of group which consistently achieves good results. This implies that group effectiveness is important and that there is a task to be accomplished which requires that people work together to ensure success. The development of an effective team can be compared with the growth of a child from infancy to adulthood. There are many steps to maturity which cannot be exactly predicted but the overall process usually goes through well-defined stages.

When a team is working well it is a creative and resourceful unit. The team has been described as 'the most powerful tool known to man'. It has the capacity to generate a uniquely stimulating, supporting and energetic climate which is enjoyed and valued by individuals and also generates achievement of a high order. Managers develop teams for several reasons.

- Team management is a positive and effective style where authoritarian approaches are no longer acceptable.
- Teams motivate and sustain their members and energise people towards achievement.
- Teams can be developed into creative problem-solving units which harness multi-disciplinary skills.
- Speedy decisions are possible using a team approach.
- Complete tasks are competently dealt with.

— Inter-personal difficulties, confusion over roles and inadequate performance are issues which are more likely to be resolved in a team.

However, the team approach is not a universal panacea for all management problems. It offers a useful tool for managing groups which have the potential to work together and accomplish common tasks. A 'team' may be defined as a group of people who directly relate together to achieve shared objectives. The need for direct relationships must be real and this effectively limits team approaches to groups with no more than ten or so members. Modified team approaches have been developed for large and less integrated groups. The case for teambuilding is potent. Many working groups are responsible for planning, innovation and sustaining a high level of output yet they fail to use the ability and competence of individual members.

The development of teams from an immature collection of squabbling individuals to a close and effective unit is often fascinating.

In essence the process requires that the group openly examines its role and functioning, identifies difficulties and learns, through experiment, how to overcome its problems. All teambuilding sessions are personal journeys as the group create a bond between one another which has an emotional dimension. Often it is possible for such ideas to be misunderstood. Deliberate teambuilding needs to be undertaken with the intention of enquiry and not as a technique for pillorying the team manager or members of the group. In medieval England vagabonds were locked in wooden restrainers known as stocks. Whilst there, local villagers would throw eggs and rotten fruit at the unfortunate people transfixed in the stocks. Teambuilding could, in malicious hands, be seen to have exactly the same function. Such an approach is potentially harmful.

Teamwork requires that everyone works for the benefit of the group, rather than the more typical style which involves scoring points and gaining personal advantage.

A team is a group of people who have a common task which needs their combined efforts. The group has a practical and emotional life of its own, and one of the distinctive features of a team is its strong sense of identity.

The test of team effectiveness is the capacity to achieve useful results. It is not easy to create a team. Relationships have to be built, work methods clarified and an energetic and positive climate created. So, effective teams have to be methodically and painstakingly constructed. It is amazing how frequently managers and team leaders fail to realise that they need to work to fashion an effective working group. They end up with squabbles, gossip circles and secret societies which fail to harness the potential of their membership.

Only the team leader, or 'team manager' as we prefer to describe the role, can initiate and sustain a teambuilding programme. The team manager takes an active role, but the exact nature will depend upon the stage of maturity of the group. Less developed groups usually require more assistance than well developed ones.

The team manager should be aware of the needs of the group and have sufficient insight into the concept of teambuilding to steer the group through a series of developmental stages. An open approach is vital. All issues affecting the group are talked through, feedback given and received, and time spent in clarifying expectations. The team manager demonstrates by his or her own behaviour the high level of openness which is an essential characteristic of the team approach.

The team manager is watchful towards team members. Their individual needs are identified and each is developed and strengthened as the work of the team continues. Outside of the team the manager is an advocate and monitors the boundaries. A close watch is kept on the relationship between the team and the surrounding organisation. The impact of the team's operations on the wider organisation is reviewed, areas for investigation, problem-solving and building better relationships are identified. One useful way to think about a team is to view it as an 'input-output' system with something coming in, being processed and emerging as a more valuable, different product at the end. The team manager often influences the inputs and the conditions in which processes occur by access to other parts of the organisation. Accordingly the team manager role requires additional skills to influence others and to gain adequate resources and support.

Some teams are much more effective than others. This can be seen most clearly on the sports field. A team of excellent individual players brought together to represent their country may fail to work as a team, and their results may then prove a national disgrace. Good teamwork requires more than individual competence, but few managers have been clearly able to identify the characteristics of an effective team.

We have studied numerous teams and analysed those which have been particularly successful. From our experience it is clear that successful teams are often those which have undergone a process of teambuilding which deals with nine key aspects of its functioning and performance. If one, or more, of these key aspects is not developed the team will fail to achieve its full potential. We call them the Building Blocks of Team Effectiveness. They are:

- clear objectives and agreed goals
- openness and confrontation
- support and trust
- co-operation and conflict
- sound procedures
- appropriate leadership
- regular review
- individual development
- sound intergroup relations.

THE NINE BUILDING BLOCKS OF TEAM EFFECTIVENESS

1   CLEAR OBJECTIVES AND AGREED GOALS

A senior management team were holding their first 'clear the air' session. The topic under discussion was deadlines for financial information. The accountant was saying how irritated he was with the way that people failed to provide the necessary data at specified times. Then someone asked him 'Why do you need this information?' He replied, 'For management information.' Then the accountant was asked, 'Who uses the information?' He replied, 'Well this team needs the information.' The team looked disbelieving then broke into laughter, and one team member said, 'For two years I believed that this information was for someone else and now I realise that it is for us. In that case, I'll do it on time and I've got some things to say about how it can be made more useful.'

Only when the objective of an activity becomes clear is it possible for people to pull together constructively and decide what is relevant and important. Many organisations demonstrate from their daily functioning that clear objectives are absent. We frequently see unhealthy competition between groups and individuals pursuing their personal goals at the expense of others.

Simply acquiring a clear definition of an objective is only a small part of the story. Until objectives are agreed they have little force. The process of agreeing objectives is frequently tedious and lengthy as apparently irrelevant objections are brought up and need to be worked through. Often people need to reconcile their own views and objectives with those of the wider organisation and this can be a difficult task. For example, we know of one person who held a responsible job as a research officer before contracting an illness which sapped her strength for years. Although she could continue to work it became her personal objective to limit her involvement so as to avoid excessive strain. The team to which she belonged, however, had different objectives which were concerned with increasing effectiveness and maximising output. In this case it became necessary to view the conflict between personal and team objectives so that creative solutions could be found to maintain team performance without undermining a team member's health.

It is a vain hope to imagine that every member of a team can be fully committed to identical objectives. Differences of opinion and conflicting interests will always exist and the most significant requirement is to develop mechanisms for exploring viewpoints, finding common ground and learning to live with differences.

Senior groups often begin a teambuilding programme with the intention of working on clarifying their objectives. The pressures on such groups can be extreme; as one manager said, 'When the alligators are snapping at your hindquarters it is hard to realise that your job is to drain the swamp.' In a complex environment where many variables remain unknown, objectives can be difficult to specify and many factors change rapidly. This places additional emphasis on the importance of team skill in setting objectives. Undeveloped teams lack the capacity to work together to take opportunities and clarify objectives in a difficult and confusing environment.

Some of the main barriers to clear objective-setting are:

1   A tendency to judge performance on the basis of personal opinion rather than measured output. People are often judged on the basis of their appearance, impact on others, attitudes, and even sex appeal. When the criteria for success are clearly identified in relation to output and judgements are clearly related to results, then thinking in terms of objectives becomes relevant and widely practised.

2   Lack of skills in objective-setting. It has been widely known for decades that objectives should, as far as possible, be (a) specific, (b) time bound and (c) measurable. Nevertheless, when managers set objectives they frequently produce vague intentions more in keeping with new year resolutions than business goals.

3   Insufficient tenacity in adhering to objectives. Interruptions and unforeseen events constantly occur and new priorities become important. Unless a firm stance is taken urgent but relatively trivial matters undermine progress towards agreed objectives.

4   Undertaking irrelevant tasks. It is sometimes easy to set an objective and then discover later that little benefit has come from effort expended. When setting a task it is helpful to ask the question 'Why?', which leads to deciding whether the objective is significant and relevant. Only when objectives can be seen to be useful should they be accepted as guidelines.

When a team possesses a clearly stated set of objectives to which all members feel committed it has achieved a great deal. Greater motiva-tion, fewer demands on management, better problem-solving and more initiatives are the desirable outcomes of clear objectives and agreed goals.

2   OPENNESS AND CONFRONTATION

Two managers were facing each other across a desk. One said, 'Henry, I really can't understand why you are so obstructive! I've asked you twenty times for that ADC 20 report and I'm still waiting. As it happens I've now got a copy through devious means.' Henry looked irritated and said, 'That's typical of you, Bill. Always going behind my back. I don't like the way that you demand everything and keep your hand close to your chest. The reason why I didn't give you the ADC 20 report is that it's not finished. You must have got the first draft.'

Their team manager was watching this exchange and he decided that the problem ought to be discussed in depth. He encouraged both men to speak their minds and describe how they saw each other. The discussion continued for half an hour as perceptions were exchanged and old wounds were brought out and displayed. At the end of the session both sat back in their chairs, sighed and grinned at each other. They knew that new difficulties would occur but had learned that they now had a greater capacity to work through difficulties and achieve constructive conclusions.

It is widely felt that conflict is a characteristic of an inadequate relationship and that mature individuals can always function together in harmony, and many people will do what they can to bury potential conflicts and inhibit their expression. Many see this as desirable because discomfort is avoided but, in reality, suppression of real conflict allows negative feelings to fester and causes a breakdown in real communication.

Teams which work well together are capable of coping with confrontation and encourage a high level of openness between team members. This quality of relationship needs to be built and reinforced by genuine feelings of support between team members. If a team is to be effective then its members need to feel able to state views, opinions, judgements, rational and irrational feelings, facts and hunches without fear of being belittled or embarrassed. Team relationships which diminish individual prestige or self-confidence result in attempts at self-protection and malicious sniping, which are real enemies of team effectiveness. When self-expression is inhibited there is often a considerable erosion of creativity and effort as more and more energy is invested in 'keeping heads down'. Effective teams are capable of tackling difficult, demanding or unpleasant issues in an open and problem-solving way.

The principles of developing openness and confrontation in a group are illustrated in the diagram below:

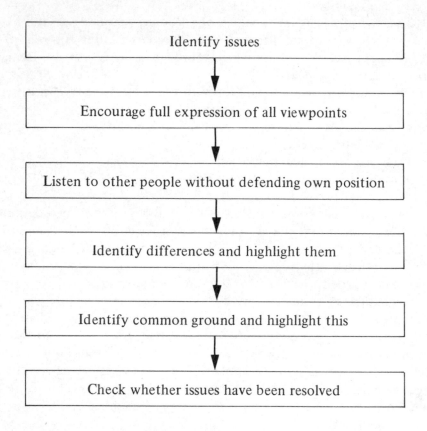

A high level of openness and confrontation are characteristics of mature relationships in all walks of life, but in working life it is not easy to achieve. Risks must be taken as people disclose information which may be contentious or may disturb the status quo. Real communication is direct, honest, and results in the development of genuine understanding of views and the sharing of experiences. One common source of inhibition is fear of the potential reaction of people with power in the team. The team manager often sets the standards of openness and confrontation, and his example is quickly identified and behaviour adjusted accordingly.

Openness and confrontation are partly stances to life and partly skills which can be learned. We can choose whether to disclose relevant information or withhold it. Our approach can also vary between straight (George Washington) and devious (James Bond).

Each approach has advantages and disadvantages which are summarised in the Table 6.

Table 6
Stances to openness

Advantages	Disadvantages
Straight	
Trusted	Exposed
Authoritative	Vulnerable
Feels strong	Cannot delude
	Can be dull
Withholding	
Not exposed	Frustrated
Difficult to attack	Ineffective
Feels self satisfied	Uncreative
Devious	
Can delude	Not trusted
Changes according	Builds resentment
to situation	Can be ineffective
Exciting	Few friends

Each person takes a personal stance towards openness, but in our experience team effectiveness is always enhanced by members deciding to be fully open — straight — and diminished by those who are withholding or devious.

The skills of openness and confrontation have much to do with 'assertion', 'active listening', and 'giving feedback'.

Assertion

The assertive person knows what he or she thinks and wants, takes definite and clear action to achieve goals and is unwilling to be sidetracked or easily defeated. Notice that we distinguish assertion from aggression which uses unfair force in an attempt to dominate. Assertion skills include clear presentation, dealing with one issue at a time, avoiding being undermined by others and seeking creative compromises. When all team members practice assertion skills there are plenty of ideas to evaluate, weak decisions are questioned and all viewpoints can be taken into account.

Active listening

Openness and confrontation are usually associated with negative feelings and viewpoints. Of course this is not always the case as it is equally important to be open about positive judgements and expressions of personal warmth. However, whether negative or positive feelings are being expressed it often happens that they are not fully heard as the receiver fails to pay attention or allow himself to absorb what is being said. The skills of active listening can be learned, although many people find them difficult to acquire. These are the key characteristics of effective listeners:

— They pay attention to what is being said.
— They suspend judgement until they have heard the 'whole story'.
— They look at the person who is talking.
— They check that they understand what is being said.
— They 'park' things in their minds and deal with them later.

Where a team practices listening skills when it meets there is a greater possibility of members openly expressing views without being prematurely judged. This leads to improved communication and a willingness to meet other people half way.

Giving feedback

As a team develops it is inevitable that people will form views of each other and operate on the assumption that their opinions are objective. It is helpful for people to express their perceptions of each other and this process has become known as 'giving feedback'. The idea fills many people with alarm as they fear that the inevitable end result must be operational mayhem and psychological carnage. Experience suggests that the opposite is the case and giving feedback strengthens individuals, relationships and overall team identity. Feedback also lends people to question their assumptions about each other and develop more realistic and deeper relationships. Good feedback can be summarised as follows:

— It is specific.
— It is descriptive.

- It clearly expresses views.
- It is timed to be near the event being discussed.
- It takes into account the needs of the receiver.
- It is checked to ensure clear communication.
- It concentrates on things the person can do something about.

When feedback is developed within a team, members can learn much from each other. Individuals who use feedback constructively have acquired a valuable asset. As team members learn to express their judgements and views they gain strength and release blocked energy. The team gains in vitality and the individuals grow in stature.

3   SUPPORT AND TRUST

A team of architects were congratulating themselves on the completion of a tender for a huge new bridge in the Middle East. The
difficulties of design had tested their skills to the utmost but the
tender was finally complete and in the envelope ready to go by
express air mail. One of the junior members seemed uncomfortable and distant. Then he said to the project leader, 'Tom, I'm
worried about those calculations I did for the supporting struts —
will you check them?' The team manager said, 'Frank, you can't
be serious! You are serious? What's the problem?' After
analysis it turned out that a relatively unimportant error had been
made but no alterations to the design were required. The tender
just made the deadline. Three months later the team were cele-
brating winning the contract and Frank, the junior architect,
said to his manager, 'Tom, I want to thank you for not ripping
me apart over that last minute recalculation on the bridge. I
thought that you would go crazy, but I really liked the way that
you didn't push me into the cesspit.' The manager said, 'Well,
Frank, if you had kept it to yourself and the bridge had fallen
down then we would all be locked in the cesspit for a hundred
years.'

Support and trust are extremely valuable characteristics of human
relationships. One of the reasons why so much business has histori-
cally been done between family relatives or within ethnic groups is
that a high level of trust has been built up. Trust becomes a valuable
commodity which enables risks to be taken that would otherwise be
avoided.

Support has been defined as 'to strengthen by assistance'. This
definition clearly makes the point that support is not a cosy and
shallow sympathy but a genuine concern to assist the other person
even if this involves giving negative feedback or facing difficult
issues. It is possible to support a person without approving of everything that he does. Conflict avoided in the name of giving support is
a short-sighted policy as relationships are built on a false foundation
of apparent warmth.

Trust usually takes a long time to develop and is not acquired
easily as it is one of the deepest of human emotions. Trust takes
time to build as it usually results from an accumulation of experiences through both good times and bad times. When we say that we
trust another person we are not saying that we can predict what they

will do, but we are usually able to predict their intentions. Our trust is that they will look after our interests and not consciously or unconsciously abuse us.

Support and trust go together as they are the bonds which link people in healthy relationships. A relationship of trust can be very vulnerable, as it can be destroyed by one malicious action or inhumane stance. Support is easier to feel but some people find it is harder to express because many social conventions inhibit the open expression of warmth.

Within a team context it is vital to develop a climate which encourages support and trust. Without support a high level of confrontation would be too harsh, whilst without trust individuals lack a willingness to disclose their true thoughts and feelings. As a team matures we see a gradual development of support and trust which are superficially present in the early stages but only become deep later in the process of team development. A fully developed team is a very close unit in which people are able to rely on each other sometimes even in matters of life or death.

Barriers to the development of support and trust are:

1   *People are not trustworthy*
    Not everyone is trustworthy or capable of giving support. Some teams contain members whose personal development has not progressed enough for them to be trusted. Where there are such members it is necessary for the issues surrounding trust to be openly confronted and worked through.

2   *Destructive competitive relationships*
    Where team members are seeking competitive advantage over each other, their relationships sometimes become characterised by showing off and point-scoring. Some lose out in the scramble for eminence and they feel second-rate citizens. People often feel very possessive and defensive about their areas of responsibility, even about the information they possess. Such competitiveness within the team can be very destructive to the development of relationships.

3   *Withholding views*
    When people refuse to express their views, others make deductions about intentions and these are usually negative. The lack of willingness to be open reduces trust and undermines supportive relationships.

4   *Imposition of goals*
When goals or standards are imposed, rather than agreed, this can easily be perceived as domineering, patronising or condescending and people feel resentful that they are being treated as mere resources rather than responsible human beings.

Within a team the qualities of high support and trust are greatly valued by members.   Where these characteristics exist, then team members will lay aside their sectional interest and strive to make the team a satisfying and effective unit.

4   CO-OPERATION AND CONFLICT

A new manager was appointed to the engineering services team in a large chemical factory. He watched the team operate for a few weeks and then called them together. He said, 'I've been watching you for several weeks and I think that there is room for improvement. It is clear that you all like and respect each other and that you are prepared to say what you think. But I'll tell you what I've noticed — you don't go out of your way to help each other. You keep in your own domains and it seems to me that you could all co-operate much more.' The team were taken aback as they had always prided themselves on their working relationships but when they discussed their work habits it became clear that they did regard each other as independent units and they could find opportunities for increased co-operation.

Co-operation can be expressed as 'working together for common gain'. This is an essential characteristic of a team approach, where the individuals put the team's objectives before their own and share in the gains and rewards from their joint activities. Co-operation implies that individuals are committed to work within a team and share their skills and information with other members. All teams require that their members devote time to forming and maintaining the health of the group. There is an element of sacrifice because each gives up some autonomy and self-interest. Committed team members feel that the goals and output of the team are important and personally satisfying. One test of team commitment is to explore how much enjoyment team members get from each other.

A mature team will pour its resources into helping a team member who is having difficulties. They will co-operate to help practically and give emotional support. A less committed team may watch a colleague in trouble with the dispassionate concern of an onlooker sitting knitting behind the guillotine during the French Revolution.

Co-operation begins when a team has clarified its goals and ensured that all its members feel that the objectives are both achievable and important. From here the team needs to develop mechanisms to enable team members to relate together during the decision-making and operational processes. Everyone is open about their need for help and about personal strengths and weaknesses. Team members watch each other's progress and are prepared to help if one member falls behind.

The team atmosphere encourages people to work with each other.

Individuals listen to the ideas of others and build on them, seeking to make the best of what is available. Morale is improved as abilities, skills and experience are utilised by the team.

As co-operation increases, the team begins to learn how to use conflict constructively and positively. Conflict is often seen as a negative characteristic which should be suppressed and avoided. However, a mature team finds way to channel conflicting ideas and viewpoints into a synthesis of ideas which has the best components of all opinions expressed. Positive conflict is exciting to experience and stimulating to the imagination. It destroys complacency and laziness as more truthful opinions are expressed.

Most teams which have demonstrated high creative capacity are able to use conflict as a tool for progress. The characteristics of these teams include:

- Lack of rigid attitudes – a preparedness exists to consider different ideas and perceptions.
- Clear presentation of ideas – divergent thoughts are clearly presented and fully expressed.
- Open reactions – team members feel free to give their honest opinions directly and forcefully.
- Techniques for conflict resolution – although conflict is encouraged, divergent ideas are related and common solutions identified.

Traditionally conflict has been seen as a negative characteristic promoted by trouble makers who are seeking personal acclaim at the expense of the team. Of course, destructive conflict is present in many relationships. However, the potential benefit from constructive conflict is great as it promotes more realistic and effective problem solving. Skills of conflict resolution can be learned and the procedures shown opposite are generally applicable.

A developed team has accomplished a high degree of co-operation which enables the resources of the group to be used for the benefit of all. When relationships do conflict, such differences are welcomed positively as they help bring creativity and realism to the group.

The main stages of conflict resolution are summarised in the following chart:

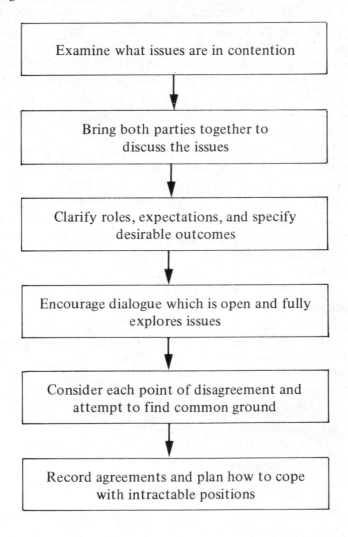

5   SOUND PROCEDURES

John's team was highly regarded. People who belonged to the team felt proud to be associated with it. Relationships were excellent and morale was outstanding. One day John was called to his senior manager's office and the boss said, 'John, I want to discuss your team, it's just not delivering the goods.' John was outraged as he felt that his team leadership goals were a model to other managers. The senior manager continued, 'The morale is excellent but, John, you and your people are simply not good at solving problems. Have a look at it and come back to me.' After a thorough diagnosis it became apparent that the team lacked sound procedures for solving problems and getting things done.

Most teams consist of individuals who have different functional or specialist responsibilities. The behaviour of each team member affects the others and procedures for clarifying roles, channelling communications and managing meetings need to be effective. It is helpful for members to discuss the team's basic organisation and assess whether their existing procedures are meeting the needs of the situation.

When a team meets together it needs to find answers to many questions and this demands good decision-making procedures and working relationships. The checklist below lists a number of crucial issues which need to be considered:

1   Is decision-making formal or informal?
2   Who has power and in what situations?
3   Are the people affected by decisions involved in the decision-making process?
4   How thorough is the information collection process?
5   Do we collect information quickly enough?
6   Is authority and responsibility matched when assignments are delegated?
7   How effectively are decisions communicated?
8   Are sufficient resources available?
9   Are resources co-ordinated?
10   Does the team set aside time to learn from experience?

Decision-making is a key aspect of the manager's job, yet the process is often done badly. Sometimes poor decision-making results from the lack of a planned systematic approach. One useful procedure for decision-making is the 'seven step approach'.

As its name implies, the seven step approach identifies seven key stages in decision-making. There is no simple format that can be mechanically applied to all problems and decisions and this approach is most useful when applied flexibly. The systematic approach is particularly useful when difficulties occur as it assists in identifying weaknesses in methodology.

SEVEN STEPS FOR SYSTEMATIC DECISION-MAKING

Step 1: Tuning In

The first requirement is to come to grips with the problem, assess its nature, understand the likely challenges and begin organising to cope with it. It is often helpful to try to identify an outline time scale and to identify whether unusual resources may be required. Each team member needs to understand the nature of the problem so that he or she can contribute fully to the decision-making process.

Step 2: Objectives

An objective is a statement of desired output. Sometimes objectives are clear and readily agreed, whilst on other occasions they are broad, hazy or contentious. An objective needs to be specific and understood by all before it can be achievable. Clarifying objectives is essential as it can prevent many of the misunderstandings and defensive arguments that result from some people not knowing what is happening.

Step 3: Success Criteria

Although objectives should be expressed in measurable terms it is useful to consider how you will monitor your progress. Two questions are useful:

— How do we measure whether we have achieved the objective?
— How do we judge whether we have worked together effectively?

When all concerned are aware of the methods of measuring success it becomes possible to use resources and time effectively. It is

particularly important to identify success criteria when unspecific
objectives are being tackled, so the statement 'to lose weight'
becomes much more useful when it is stated as 'to lose one pound
in weight each week for three months'.

Step 4: Information

Most problems need to be understood in depth before a solution can
be found. People have opinions, feelings, facts, ideas and prejudices
to contribute. Certain kinds of problems may involve research or
data collection outside the team. All this information needs to be
collected and made sense of to provide the basis for informed
decision-making. Unfortunately, the human brain cannot work
with too much data at any one time, so skilful techniques of display-
ing information greatly aid recognition of key issues and choices.
When the necessary information has been collected different choices
and options need to be identified and their merits explored.

Step 5: Planning

The planning stage begins with a decision about what is to be done.
For example, in pursuit of the objective 'to make £10000 ($20000)
by Christmas' we may have identified three options:

    (a)   become a tennis star;
    (b)   sell newspapers in the street; or
    (c)   make a successful pop record.

The planning stage begins with our choice which may be to 'sell
newspapers in the street'. Then we must decide

    What is to be done?
    When is it to be done?
    How is it to be done?
    Where is it to be done?
    What we need to do to make it happen?
    How we are going to control it?

For action to be successful each person involved needs to be able to
visualise clearly what is to be done and to identify their role.

Step 6: Action

It has been said that there is no substitute for getting things done.
Most decisions are taken because something needs to happen

differently. If all the preceeding five stages have been thoroughly undertaken the team will have the best chance of achieving a successful outcome. The quality of performance is largely a function of the quality of preparation, with, perhaps, a little bit of luck thrown in for good measure.

Step 7: Review to Improve

We learn from seeing the results of our actions. As we examine the factors which led to success and failure we have a most valuable opportunity for learning and personal growth. Accordingly, the final stage of a systematic problem-solving and decision-making cycle is deliberately to set aside time to review performance with the intention of learning from the experience. It is important to avoid becoming dispirited or pessimistic as sometimes the most disastrous happenings provide us with highly significant learning. Without feedback there is little chance of changing and developing.

At certain times in the decision-making cycle the group may choose to use a consensus approach to pool the maximum number of ideas and gain maximum commitment. Consensus is a difficult approach to decision-making. At best it offers an excellent opportunity to collect ideas, clarify objectives and plan coherent action. At worst, consensus-seeking is an excuse for muddled decision-making and poor morale.

Here are some guidelines which may help you to improve the quality of consensus groups:

Ground rules
— Identify basic ground rules.
— Stress importance of reasoning.
— Avoid people arguing for their own views at expense of group.
— Seek to identify logic.

Individual positions
— Ask people to clarify their 'going-in' positions.
— Be explicit about assumptions.
— Clarify where each person stands.

Clarify objectives
— Try to explore objectives.

— Work hard to share objectives.
— Record statement of objectives.

Handling information
— Use a visual display of data.
— Try to visualise suggestions to test them.
— Explore understanding of the problem.

Listening
— Try to hear each other.
— Avoid over-talking.
— Avoid premature judgement.

Assertion
— Help less assertive people.
— Be intolerant of aggression.
— Avoid being sidetracked.
— Clearly state views.

Co-ordination
— Leader must be skilful.
— Periodic summaries help.
— Leader organises group to tackle problem.

If you get stuck
— Try reviewing objectives.
— Clarify issue in dispute.
— Assemble data.
— Try to make most probable deduction.
— Collect new data if necessary.

The manager or team leader is the key man in determining the degree to which the team will participate in decision-making. There are four approaches which can be used:

I take the decisions: The leader retains control and feels no obligation to consult.
I will seek your opinion and then decide: The leader makes the decisions after discussing the topic with team members.
I will choose others to help me in taking decisions: The leader selects others to assist him in decision-making.
We will take decisions: The problem is brought before the team who discuss it and jointly solve the problem.

Effective decision-making in teams requires sound information handling, communication and skilful problem-solving. It is important that procedures are reviewed and challenged from time to time as they can become fossilised. The team must continue to seek simple and effective procedures that enable the maximum return from available resources.

6   APPROPRIATE LEADERSHIP

An American enterprise engaged in the micro-chip business having expanded rapidly had decided to open an office in Europe. The marketing vice-president commissioned an extensive survey and judged that Hamburg would be the best location. He joined the corporation president for a planning meeting and found the chief executive reading his report. The president said, 'I like the concept, Hal, but why Hamburg?' The marketing vice-president replied, 'To me the logic suggests that Hamburg will be the most convenient location.' The president sat back in his chair and said, 'Well, my philosophy is to give a man his head. Some people will make it work from a hut in Tahiti whilst others will fail even though they have all the resources imaginable. First choose the man and then find the location. Of course, it has to be sensible, but if you get the right guy to head it up, then he'll make it work.'

The president was talking about leadership, which is a crucial quality in organisational life. An effective leader makes best use of resources and develops competence and capability. An ineffective leader squanders potential and misplaces effort. Organisational effectiveness depends greatly on the quality of leadership.

In recent years we have begun to understand leadership behaviour more clearly. It was apparent that some individuals were excellent leaders in one situation but completely unable to cope in a different context. We can now identify with precision the skills of leadership and when a particular kind of leadership is appropriate.

Studies of leadership have determined that leaders perform two vital functions: whilst influencing people in what to do and controlling situations, they develop good relationships and encourage participation.

It has been shown that people need different kinds of leadership according to their ability and attitude. When there is low ability or low willingness to perform a task it is necessary for the leader to spend a lot of time in controlling and directing. However, where there is greater ability and willingness to perform, a leader will encourage individuals by increasing participation and involvement.

Studies have shown that always the most important factor was the character of the group or individual being led. It seemed that a style of management would work well in one setting but not in another. In other words there was no single best approach which could be used universally. The leader who used an appropriate style for a particular group was the person who would most often succeed in achieving high output.

Other studies have tried to analyse situations to see whether it was possible to identify key characteristics. Work by two Americans, Paul Hersey and Kenneth Blanchard[3] took this much further. These two researchers hit upon the idea of relating style to the degree to which subordinates were capable and felt comfortable about tackling the job in hand. This measurement of 'maturity' could be carried out quite scientifically; at the lowest level it was defined as unwilling and unable, whilst the most mature people were defined as willing and able.

Linking these two ideas together, it became apparent that the manager dealing with an unwilling and unable group needs to spend a lot of time clarifying goals and simply telling people what needs to be done. ('Telling')

As the group develops, so they require to get to know him or her as a person, and become interested in the work and the people around them. ('Selling')

Later, as they become more mature, so the wish for participation and involvement grows. The group can be left much more to tend to their own affairs. They still need help and direction, but not the same energy or control which was present earlier. They have grown beyond this. ('Participating')

At the fourth stage, group members are largely self-directed, as they organise their own affairs. Here the management style appropriate to the situation is characterised by delegation. The manager can trust his or her subordinates to get on with the problem in hand. This leaves time to tackle other jobs, such as planning and representing the group outside. ('Delegating')

Teams go through a number of development stages and the effective leader helps the group progress to a high level of responsibility and competence. This means that he needs:

- to know where the team is at the moment
- to know how the team is likely to progress
- to know what he can do to help.

Teams can be viewed as being in one of these four positions:

(D) Willing and able

(C) Receptive and able

(B) Receptive but unable

(A) Unwilling and unable

Teams develop slowly and can lapse. However, almost all can be helped and encouraged to progress to a higher level of maturity. As control and instruction are decreased, so the behaviour of the group needs to be watched to see that they take responsibility and perform well. The diagram below shows the process.

THE LEADERSHIP STYLE BALANCE

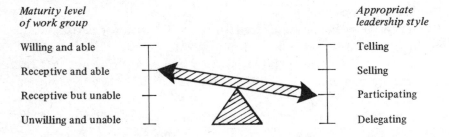

Maturity level of work group		Appropriate leadership style
Willing and able		Telling
Receptive and able		Selling
Receptive but unable		Participating
Unwilling and unable		Delegating

Gradually, the balance shifts as the team becomes more responsible and capable. Ultimately, the team becomes capable of handling its own internal management and problems.

Not all teams need leaders of a permanent nature, as many mature teams are able to change their leadership to suit circumstances. High team maturity can be judged by such things as:

    — high level of achievement
    — open and friendly relations between team members
    — capacity to undertake assignments without help
    — shrewd use of available resources
    — capacity to deal with uncertainty
    — rapid reaction to new circumstances
    — high level of energy

   — good mix of individual skills and personalities
   — effective problem solving procedures.

With the development of team competence it becomes possible for the team manager to delegate important areas of responsibility. Delegation is not only a way of enabling a manager to devote more time to other issues; it is also recognition of the ability and maturity of others. Often a low level of delegation results from lack of trust in subordinates, insufficient time spent in training and development activities and excessive involvement with the hectic but trivial events of the moment. Delegation should enhance rather than threaten the manager's status. Any manager who claims that he is indispensable should question whether he is not avoiding developing his subordinates to their full potential.

Delegation can be defined as 'passing responsibility for the completion of tasks downwards'. However, the person to whom work is delegated must have sufficient initiative to change course, according to circumstances. Simply telling someone to undertake a task is not real delegation as genuine discretion has to be exercised.

Many managers find it difficult to delegate as they fear that important aspects of the job will be neglected or bungled. However, the benefits are clear:

   — less strain on the manager
   — better use of team resources
   — genuine development of subordinates
   — quicker decision-making
   — better use of time
   — more creativity
   — improvement in morale.

Despite the potential pitfalls, the case for delegation is overwhelming. It could be described as the ultimate style of leadership where work is being completed without the need for control or support.

Effective delegation is based on the following principles:

1   An analysis of areas of accountability and identification of tasks that can be delegated
2   Consideration of the present maturity level of each team member and training to develop their competence
3   Progressive assignment of tasks to build a more responsible work load
4   Regular counselling and review

5   Emphasis on clarifying objectives and establishing success
     criteria.

There are often risks in delegation, but if these are intelligently
managed the leader reaps high rewards.

Effective leadership is essential for the development of teamwork.
When a team manager lacks the ability or skills to develop a team
approach it is probable that the potential of the group will never be
exploited. One of the most important leadership functions is to provide opportunities for important issues to be clarified and worked
through to a satisfactory resolution. Teams grow in stature as they
confront issues and deal with them. This can be done by setting a
personal example, demonstrating openness in practice. Once
barriers have been broken through, the release of energy and greater
depth of relationships more than outweigh any discomfort experienced. Individuals are brought together, objectives clarified,
relationships built in a confronting yet supportive climate, and
satisfying and effective work methods are developed. The most
respected leaders are those who are authentic because it is almost
always disastrous to 'play a leadership role' rather than be oneself.

The effective team leader:

- is in touch with his own energy and stimulates others
- has studied team development and can aid his group progress
- adopts an open approach which builds trust
- develops an authentic style
- affirms a positive view of human nature
- is clear about the standards he wishes to achieve
- is receptive to people's hopes, fears, problems and dignity
- faces facts honestly and squarely
- tries to make the work place happy, satisfying and
  interesting.

7 REGULAR REVIEW

A group of senior managers were reviewing how they could communicate reorganisation plans to a workforce of thousands. They
knew that many would feel threatened or angry by the inevitable
changes, and they wanted to put a clear and convincing case to each
employee. In the end it was decided that a special video film would
be made which would be shown in every factory and office. Senior
managers gathered in a studio and made their presentations to the
video cameras. They immediately went and watched their efforts
and at the end of the viewing the chief executive said, 'We've got to
do a lot better than that. It's boring and confusing. Let's analyse
where we are going wrong and try again.' They repeated this cycle
four times and ultimately were satisfied. The film was seen by every
company employee and the reorganisation plans were accepted.

Regular review of performance is essential to the development of
competence. Sports teams are well aware of the need for review and
spend hours discussing their successes and failures. They identify
strengths and weaknesses and plan strategies for improvement.

The most valuable reviews incorporate objective and impartial
data. A team will gain from periodic reflection on its performance
and a dispassionate enquiry into missed opportunities and inadequate
performance. Some teams appear to operate an informal conspiracy
to avoid self-reflection and review. There are several possible reasons
for this reluctance to review :

> *Politeness* — Team members feel that it is not appropriate to
> make personal comments about each other.
> *Fear of hurting others* — Concern that negative criticism may be
> damaging.
> *Lack of trust* — The team lacks positive relationships which
> permit frank exchange.
> *Protection of the status quo* — A belief that existing successes
> may be damaged by open criticism.
> *Poor skills* — Team members lack skills in self expression and
> analysis.

Regular review helps a team to evolve towards maturity. Usually
we find that teams spend far too little time reviewing their effectiveness. It is often easy for each team meeting to finish with a review of
effectiveness, and perhaps with regular teambuilding sessions, looking
at broader aspects of team functioning.

There are many different approaches and aids to team review and once the skills of review are learned they become part of the way of life of the team. Here are some key techniques which have proved useful in practice.

Using an observer

A team will often benefit from using an impartial observer who sits ouside of the group. Often he will have a check list which helps him to analyse behaviour and give feedback to the group. He is really looking for those acts or words which helped the team in its task and those which hindered the achievement of objectives. The observer will be careful to avoid forming judgements and colouring the facts with his own prejudices. At a suitable point, the observer will be invited to report to the group and his comments will then form the basis of a discussion.

Using closed-circuit television

In the hands of someone who is both a skilled observer and a skilled operator of CCTV equipment, the video tape can be a most useful tool. The group can replay sections of its own activity and analyse in depth what happened and why. All are able to see for themselves how they behaved and each individual can assess his or her personal contribution to team effectiveness. In this way learning can be greatly speeded up and difficult issues identified, confronted and worked through.

Using team surveys

A wide range of team surveys are available to enable a team to monitor its own performance and set goals for its improvement. It is helpful for the team to identify potential weaknesses and devise a method for systematic review. Objectives can then be established for the improvement of performance and regular checks made on team effectiveness. Regular review has the following benefits:

- ensures that adequate effort is directed towards planning
- decision-making processes are improved
- support, trust and openness increase
- individuals improve their contributions
- meetings become more productive and enjoyable
- involvement and commitment increase.

The process of review is a vital stage in developing team effectiveness, yet we often see this step omitted as the pressures of daily life keep the team in a frenzy of activity. In the long term, however, time must be found to step back and consider the team's behaviour with an impartial but critical eye.

8   *INDIVIDUAL DEVELOPMENT*

A group of hospital administrators were facing a difficult dilemma. They were suffering from a shortage of money and staff and had to reduce the quality of care given to patients. All those present in the meeting had views about where they felt that economies could be made. One man, responsible for technical equipment, contributed little to the discussion, and gradually it was decided that his department should bear the brunt of the financial economies. The meeting was concluded and most of the managers left feeling satisfied. The technical manager, however, said to a colleague, 'You know, Tom, I feel badly about this. We've got our priorities all wrong. My department is taking far too big a share of the economies.' His colleague asked, 'Why didn't you speak out?' After a long pause the reply came, 'I don't know, I guess I'm poor at expressing myself.'

This manager contributed poorly to the team because he was an undeveloped individual. The purpose of teamwork is to pool the skills of individuals and so produce a better result than that which individuals could achieve. The effectiveness of a team should be greater than the sum of its parts but, of course, teams need to pay attention to the development of individual skills and abilities, because these are the raw materials. When a person contributes weakly, the overall output of the team is diminished.

Individual development is a fascinating topic and a new analysis[4] of individual capacity has identified eleven key problems or 'blockages', widely experienced by those in management jobs. These are:

1   *Self-management incompetence*
    Being unable to make the most of one's time, energy and skill or being unable to cope with the stresses of present day managerial life.
2   *Unclear personal values*
    Being unclear about one's own values or having values which are inappropriate to working and private life in the 1980s.
3   *Confused personal goals*
    Being unclear about one's personal life or work goals or having goals which are incompatible with work and life in the 1980s.
4   *Stunted personal development*
    Lacking the stance, ability and receptiveness to rise to new

challenges and opportunities.

5 *Inadequate problem-solving skills*
Lacking the problem-solving and decision-making strategies and abilities necessary to solve the problems of the 1980s.

6 *Low creativity*
Lacking the ability to generate sufficient new ideas to keep ahead, or to capitalise on them.

7 *Low influence*
Having insufficient influence to gain commitment and help from others or to affect their decisions.

8 *Lack of managerial insight*
Having insufficient understanding of the motivation of people at work or having values about the leadership of others which are out-dated, inhumane or inappropriate.

9 *Poor supervisory skills*
Lacking the practical ability to achieve results through the efforts of others.

10 *Low trainer ability*
Lacking the ability or willingness to help others to grow and expand their capacity.

11 *Low teambuilding ability*
Being unable to help groups or teams to develop and become more effective.

When new members join a team it is important that they are introduced with understanding but also made to realise that high standards of performance are expected. A well-developed team member is one who:

— listens to others
— learns from experience
— is prepared to be open about his position
— will change a viewpoint through reason but not through bullying
— is willing to take reasonable risks
— develops good relations with others
— has sufficient personal energy
— assertively present his case.

Individual development needs to be much more comprehensive than many conventional management textbooks suggest.

Business life is full of countless examples of executives who seem to have all the right skills and all the knowledge, technical and otherwise, and yet still never seem to achieve worthwhile results. We also meet many executives, particularly owner-managers who have had little training and on the surface appear deficient in the accepted managerial skills, and yet they have created immensely successful businesses and seem to have the knack of always succeeding.

In practice, management is about seeing opportunities, seizing them and making things happen, and some people seem able to do that continually. Observers have noticed that the most effective and the least effective almost invariably display two different sets of characteristics.

The less effective seem to have a passive approach to life wishing to be undisturbed as much as possible. They find challenge frightening and avoid it whenever possible. They also avoid insight into themselves and their beliefs. They do not welcome feedback from others and criticism, far from being perceived as healthy, is seen as unhelpful and threatening. They are not in touch with their own feelings, and do not wish to be, and new experiences are avoided because of the threat which they could bring. Often they try to manipulate people and seldom do they seek to increase the freedom of others. They lack concern for others and whilst they may give sympathy to them they rarely offer real help. Their beliefs are the beliefs of others, often learned in childhood and seldom seriously questioned; they are not authentic people. They are intolerant of divergent views and are often heard to bemoan the fact that others are not like them. In their unrelaxed posture towards life they are content with low standards. When difficult problems arise they are the first to shun responsibility. For them life would be happier if they were surrounded by weak people, but they are not and so often they resent the strong whom they see contributing substantially to their unhappy and unsatisfactory lives.

Successful people by contrast seem to have an active approach to life. They are the people who make things happen and are constantly seeking new challenges for themselves and the groups which they represent. They wish to know more about themselves and are interested in the feedback which others can give them about both their strengths and their weaknesses. They welcome constructive criticism. They recognise that time and energy are limited in terms of human existence and, seeing them as man's most valuable resources, they plan their lives to make the most of them. They constantly seek new experiences because they see the quality of life being linked to an expanding range of experience. By constantly achieving good results they build a reputation as people who can be relied upon to 'come up with the goods', and they are committed to seeing things through even when difficult situations arise. They understand their own feelings and try to use them as a positive force in their relationships with others. They care about others and their feelings and whilst they may not always agree they remain tolerant to the beliefs of those around them. They strive to be open with others, for they have nothing to hide and they realise that honesty is a much neglected value but is usually the best course. They are not frightened to give freedom to others, realising that this is vital for personal growth. They set high standards for themselves and the groups which they represent and are constantly seeking opportunities to extend themselves and their colleagues. Because they have worked things through for themselves they are clear about their own beliefs and are not inhibited by the teachings of others. Because they are successful they are strong and they rejoice in that strength, using it as a positive force for themselves and their colleagues. They are relaxed, happy people who see life as an adventure which they enjoy immensely.

Very few people conform totally with either of these sets of characteristics; it is a question of degree, and individual development is essentially about which set of characteristics we move towards and which we move away from. The two sets of characteristics when placed side by side become stark alternatives; choices which we are able to make about ourselves, our approach to life and our approach to work. Often those individuals who predominantly exhibit the high effectiveness characteristics are uncomfortable people to work with, their drive and dynamism at first sight appearing to inhibit the common good of the team. The really effective teams, however, learn to capitalise on these qualities and encourage their less effective members to move towards them.

9   SOUND INTER-GROUP RELATIONS

A medium-sized company had developed two sales teams. One, 'Dawnfresh Products', sold fresh vegetables to hotels and hospitals whilst the second, 'Dawnfresh Retail', serviced many thousands of small shops. Between these two groups a rivalry developed which gradually poisoned their relationship and co-operation. Each saw the other as arrogant, selfish and negative. The sales director watched the deterioration of this relationship and decided that it was damaging the effectiveness of his function. After discussing with a consultant it was decided to bring both groups together and try to 'lance the boil'. The day came and both teams sat looking at each other. The consultant suggested that each group, privately, select ten adjectives which they considered described the other group. Ten minutes were allowed for this task. When the lists were shared there was a stunned silence. Both groups were annoyed by the vehemence and hostility shown by the other team's adjectives. They began a furious exchange, and months of pent up aggression were expressed. Gradually the excitement cooled and the groups were more able to look at their relationship from a realistic and balanced perspective. Finally they agreed to try to co-operate more and made plans to communicate more openly, and then they retired together to the bar for a few drinks.

Groups frequently develop inaccurate or negative views about each other. This can often be seen vividly between communities, as in the case of the Protestants and Catholics in Northern Ireland, or between nations, as with the Arab/Israeli conflict. Each develops a mental picture of the other and forms judgements about qualities and merit. Such perceptions often prejudice open and constructive relationships. If we look at the behaviour of early man when hunting bands and tribal loyalties governed relationships, then we can perhaps see how we learned to be suspicious of members of other groups, and developed the habit of strengthening our own group at the expense of others.

A small enterprise, in the pioneer stage, may function as a single team. However, with the growth of organisation, functional teams form, rather like cells dividing, to form a more complex organism. At this stage of development the senior team will seek to clarify overall objectives, but may well find that separate teams are unwilling to communicate or co-operate fully.

Inter-team relations often need to be consciously developed

particularly where daily routines fail to provide sufficient contact to establish a rapport. Many managers fail to perceive the need for deliberate 'bridge building' between groups but usually much can be done to improve co-operation.

Inter-team relations are an important area because almost always teams need to co-operate together to achieve common objectives. Whilst often it seems that there is a natural force pulling a team together, it also often appears that there is an equally natural force which polarises teams. Indeed, some teams develop increased coherence by demonstrating their superiority above other groups. This has many negative effects for the wider organisation.

Groups frequently engage in negative competition which can be observed as a subtle undercurrent, expressed through negative comments, sarcastic remarks and the absence of open communication. Managers often talk about their jobs in terms borrowed from sport. They talk of 'scoring points', 'playing to win' and 'knowing the rules of the game'. Such expressions indicate how some team leaders think about their jobs. The images of 'winning' which we learn as children usually persist into adult life. So we may see one team succeeding whilst another fails. Teams rarely develop a real depth of communication with other teams.

The key symptoms of poor inter-group relations are:

- negative attitudes and 'sniping'
- little co-operative contact
- ponderous project work
- personalities unknown to others
- lack of shared objectives
- superior attitudes and destructive rivalry.

Psychological studies using the transactional analysis framework observe many 'games' and destructive strategies between teams. For example, it is not unknown for one team deliberately to cause another team to lose face by playing 'Now I've got you, you son of a bitch'.[5]

There are ways to improve inter-group relations which can be undertaken by any manager in the daily routines of his job. These suggestions may appear mundane, but they frequently result in tangible benefit:

1 Ensure that the actions and decisions of the team are communicated and understood.

2   Recognise that although teams are not the same that is no reason for them to stay apart.

3   Try to understand the other team's point of view, recognising their problems and difficulties and offering a hand of friendship when needed.

4   Continually seek out ways of working effectively with others.

5   Don't be too rigid in defending team boundaries.

6   Recognise that boundaries and responsibilities between teams will need to be reviewed and amended from time to time.

7   Anticipate and eliminate potential inter-team problems before they arise.

8   Really try to listen to others and do all that is possible to help them listen to you.

9   Use others as a source of ideas and comparison.

10 Understand and utilise differences in people.

11 Make a point of joining the other team members for lunch/drinks.

12 Take active steps to find out what others teams do.

13 Hold periodic liaison meetings.

14 Try to find opportunities to help other teams in practical ways.

15 Make requests for help or information clearly and specifically.

One simple but useful technique for improving inter-group relations is called 'role negotiation'. Each team produces a written answer under four headings:

1   What things we would like you to do more of or do better.
2   What things we would like you to do less or stop doing.
3   What things we would like you to begin to do that you do not do now.
4   What things you do which we would like to continue.

The teams share these lists and begin to discuss how their co-operation can be improved.

Once achieved, effective inter-group relationships bring a host of advantages. Amongst the foremost of these are greater ability to influence the organisation, more available help, easier flow of information, easier problem-solving, less anxiety and happier, more enjoyable working lives.

Inter-group relations improve over time. Once a good rapport is established people tend to enjoy contact and find ways to increase co-operation and interaction. The basic characteristics of good inter-team relations are similar to those within a good team. In particular, trust, openness, confrontation and sound procedures are extremely important. In addition, it is important for each team to understand not only its own role within the wider organisation but also the roles of other teams. Sound inter-group relations build a supportive climate between groups, pull divergent threads together and increase overall effectiveness.

PRACTICAL TEAMBUILDING

These then are the raw materials which can be used to build effective teams. Teams which are open and confronting, whose members support and trust each other, who use co-operation and conflict wisely, who have sound procedures and appropriate leadership, who review to improve, who place a high priority on the development of members and who have sound relations with other groups are the ones most likely to succeed. The principal purpose of this book is to help you to take the strategic decisions which are necessary before teambuilding commences and to introduce you to the building blocks of effective teamwork.

If you decide to embark on teambuilding, you will probably want some practical help and advice on how to begin. There are many books around to help you and we have set down our ideas and experiences in two of them. They are:

Team Development Manual – Mike Woodcock
Appealing particularly to managers and trainers, this is the companion volume to *Organisation Development Through Teambuilding*. This manual contains all the elements required for a complete team-development programme, together with guidance enabling the user to construct one to suit his own needs. Much of the manual consists of material which can be directly used in training, including nine 'lecturettes' explaining the key concepts, forty-five 'activities', and many model training programmes. One particularly useful feature is a diagnostic instrument that allows the manager or trainer to identify his team's specific weaknesses and then to select the most appropriate activities for overcoming them. There is also a section listing sources of further help.

CONTENTS

Preface

PART I   IMPROVING TEAMWORK
What is teamwork?
The stages of team development
The limitations of teambuilding
Diagnosing teamwork problems
Action planning
Groundrules for team development
Designing teambuilding events
Selecting teambuilding activities

PART II   TEAMBUILDING RESOURCES
Practical activities
Lecturettes on teambuilding theory

PART III   FURTHER INFORMATION
Reading list
Films and tapes
Consultants
Other useful organisations

Publishers: Gower, Aldershot, 1979; Halsted, New York, 1979.

Improving Work Groups – Dave Francis and Don Young
Appealing particularly to the professional adviser and consultant, this draws clearly on the practical teambuilding work of the authors.

CONTENTS

PART I   THE TEAM BUILDING PROCESS
How to use this book
Team building: what, why, how
What is a team?
What is team building?
Why do it?
How to start team building
How to manage the team-building process
The team-development consultant

PART II   THE TEAM REVIEW QUESTIONNAIRE
Analyzing the team-review questionnaire

PART III   GENERATING TEAM DEVELOPMENT
   I   Effective leadership
  II   Suitable membership
 III   Team commitment
  IV   Team climate
   V   Team achievement
  VI   Corporate role
 VII   Work methods
VIII   Team organisation
  IX   Critiquing
   X   Individual development
  XI   Creative capacity
 XII   Intergroup relations

PART IV   BUILDING STRENGTHS AND CLEARING BLOCKAGES
Tools for team building
What to do when: an activity index
Activities

Publishers: University Associates, La Jolla, California, 1979.

NOTES

1 Woodcock, M., *Team Development Manual*; Gower, Aldershot, 1979; Halsted, New York, 1979. Francis, D. and Young, D., *Improving Work Groups*, University Associates, 1979.
2 See *Team Development Manual.*
3 Hersey, P. and Blanchard, K.H., *Management of Organisational Behaviour and Utilizing Human Resources*, Prentice Hall, 1977.
4 Francis, D. and Woodcock, M., *The Unblocked Boss*, University Associates, 1981.
5 Berne, Eric, *Games People Play: The Psychology of Human Relationships*, Grove Press Inc., 1964.